Series / Number 07-075

# METRIC SCALING
## Correspondence
## Analysis

**SUSAN C. WELLER**
*University of Texas*

**A. KIMBALL ROMNEY**
*University of California*

**SAGE** PUBLICATIONS
*The International Professional Publishers*
Newbury Park   London   New Delhi

CALS
H61.27
.W45
1990

*For information address:*

SAGE Publications, Inc.
2111 West Hillcrest Drive
Newbury Park, California 91320

SAGE Publications Ltd.
28 Banner Street
London EC1Y 8QE
England

SAGE Publications Pvt. Ltd.
M-32 Market
Greater Kailash I
New Delhi 110 048 India

Printed in the United States of America

International Standard Book Number 0-8039-3750-4

Library of Congress Catalog Card No. 90-8731

**FIRST PRINTING, 1990**
Sage Production Editor: Susan McElroy

When citing a university paper, please use the proper form. Remember to cite the current Sage University Paper series title and include the paper number. One of the following formats can be adapted (depending on the style manual used):

(1) WELLER, S. C., & ROMNEY, A. K. (1990) Metric Scaling: Correspondence Analysis. Sage University Paper Series on Quantitative Applications in the Social Sciences, 07-075. Newbury Park, CA: Sage.

*OR*

(2) Weller, S. C., & Romney, A. K. (1990). *Metric scaling: Correspondence analysis* (Sage University Paper series on Quantitative Applications in the Social Sciences, series no. 07-075). Newbury Park, CA: Sage.

# CONTENTS

## SERIES EDITOR'S INTRODUCTION

When data analysts turn to examine systematically the relationships among a set of variables, they may be bewildered by the large array of techniques to choose from. Drs. Weller and Romney offer a possible prescription, by focusing the choice on three leading approaches to metric scaling. A traditional method, *principal components analysis* (PCA), serves as a base of comparison for the more recent techniques of *multidimensional preference scaling* (MDPREF) and, particularly, the increasingly popular *correspondence analysis* (CA). Although these techniques can yield similar results, there are differences worth noting. MDPREF and CA are especially advantaged over PCA, in that relationships among measures and objects (among column and row variables) can be presented in the same space. Consider an example.

Suppose Prof. Apple, a community sociologist, administered an attitude survey on 20 public issues to the 15 members of Middleberg City Council. On the basis of a PCA (the usual column variable variety), she produces a figure showing that issues seem to "load" on two dimensions, one she labels "fiscal" and the other "welfare." What she would like to go on to do is show, in a single figure, how issues relate to each other, and how the council members relate to the issues. (She suspects the Democrats on the council are closer to the "welfare" dimension.) Therefore, she carries out MDPREF and CA, obtaining two illustrations of this joint configuration. Both suggest that the members of the council do, indeed, separate themselves by parties as well as by issues. The picture from the two procedures appears similar, but not identical, because the variables were standardized differently. (Moreover, the MDPREF pictorial representation is a "vector" model, whereas that of CA is a "point" model.)

Weller and Romney explain how to conduct and interpret these scaling procedures, with the copious use of figures and examples — about the color receptors of goldfish, home finances in a rural Guatemalan village, contraceptive methods use, SES and mental health, chronological seriation, English kinship terms. In addition, they extend the application of CA to contingency tables, rank-ordered data, and multiway data. Although correspondence analysis is already getting a fair amount of attention in anthropology and sociology, this introductory monograph should make the technique appreciated and accessible to a still wider social science audience.

*— Michael S. Lewis-Beck*
Series Editor

# METRIC SCALING
## Correspondence Analysis

**SUSAN C. WELLER**
*University of Texas*

**A. KIMBALL ROMNEY**
*University of California*

## 1. INTRODUCTION

The aim of this monograph is to present a set of closely related techniques that facilitate the exploration and display of a wide variety of multivariate data, both categorical and continuous. Our attention is focused on the descriptive task of revealing the structure of the data and providing a scaled model of that structure.

All sciences deal with discovering and modeling the relationships among objects and variables. In this monograph we focus on representing the relations among two or more sets of variables. The aim is to summarize and reveal mutual relationships among variables of different kinds. Most of the applications are exploratory in nature rather than predictive. Attention is focused on the interrelations among all the variables without regard to such distinctions as *dependent* versus *independent* variables.

The tasks of measuring and classifying subjects, attributes of subjects, responses to questionnaires, behavioral responses, demographic characteristics, and so on, are present in almost all social science research. The methods that are presented in this monograph are meant to aid in these tasks by summarizing complex relationships among many subjects and many sets of variables simultaneously.

### Some Sample Results

It is useful to illustrate the methods by presenting the results from a small data set. This will illustrate graphically what can be expected of

AUTHORS' NOTE: *We would like to acknowledge the comments of Roy D'Andrade, Dan Dalton, Joel Harrison, Michael Lewis-Beck, Alaina Michaelson, Kenneth Small, and two anonymous reviewers. We would also like to thank Anne Turner and Kandy Burke.*

the methods before discussing theoretical aspects of the models and outlining the details of how computations are performed. The example we use comes from a study of the color vision receptors in goldfish.

Schiffman and Falkenberg (1968) analyzed data on color vision in the cones of goldfish retina collected originally by Marks (1965).

> Marks presented his data in the form of spectral absorption curves for single cones, where the abscissa was the wavelength of the light stimulus and the ordinate the amount of absorption. To obtain these curves he recorded the amount of light absorbed by single cones for all wavelengths. . . . By measuring the amount of absorption for nine particular wavelengths for eleven cones a data matrix was produced. The order of the stimuli and the receptors has been randomized to simulate the conditions of unknown stimulus and receptor properties. (Schiffman and Falkenberg, 1968: 199)

One of the primary questions is to ascertain whether there seem to be distinct types of receptor cones and, if so, how many. Next, we might ask about the scaling of the colors and determine if they are arranged in an interpretable way. A final question would focus on how the type of receptor cone relates to color stimuli, that is, do different types of cones have special affinities for different color wavelengths?

In the next few pages we will present several ways of examining the structure of the data reported by Schiffman and Falkenberg (1968: 199) and presented in Table 1.1. At this point we want to illustrate the possible utilities of the various methods without going into the underlying theory or method of computation for each. The methods are all closely interrelated and therefore we expect the various results to be consistent with one another although each displays a somewhat distinct perspective.

The first step in any analysis is to inspect the raw data by eye to form some notion of the possible information it contains. As the analysis proceeds one should always link the abstract representations to what is visible in the raw data. If one understands a little about the data from inspection it can save one from gross errors in interpretation. Inspection of the data and linking what it indicates to an abstract representation will frequently save one a great deal of difficulty. For example, an examination of the data in Table 1.1 reveals that rows 11 and 10 at the bottom of the table seem quite similar to each other. Rows 3 and 2 are also similar to each other but very distinct from rows 11 and 10. Thus in any representation of the similarity of rows one would expect rows 11 and 10 to be close together and fairly distant from rows 3 and 2.

TABLE 1.1

Marks's Data on Receptor Cone Sensitivity to Color Stimuli

| Receptor Cone | Green 530 | Yellow 585 | Red 660 | Blue-1 458 | Bl-Gr 498 | Blue 485 | Green 540 | Orange 610 | Violet 430 |
|---|---|---|---|---|---|---|---|---|---|
| 7 | 97 | 137 | 45 | 2 | 52 | 46 | 106 | 92 | 14 |
| 4 | 154 | 93 | 0 | 101 | 140 | 122 | 153 | 44 | 99 |
| 1 | 12 | 0 | 0 | 153 | 57 | 89 | 4 | 0 | 147 |
| 5 | 152 | 116 | 26 | 85 | 127 | 103 | 148 | 75 | 46 |
| 9 | 86 | 139 | 146 | 59 | 52 | 58 | 79 | 163 | 87 |
| 6 | 151 | 109 | 0 | 78 | 121 | 85 | 154 | 57 | 73 |
| 8 | 84 | 151 | 120 | 65 | 73 | 77 | 102 | 154 | 44 |
| 3 | 14 | 0 | 0 | 152 | 100 | 125 | 0 | 0 | 145 |
| 2 | 32 | 23 | 0 | 154 | 75 | 110 | 24 | 17 | 153 |
| 11 | 55 | 120 | 132 | 0 | 39 | 40 | 62 | 147 | 0 |
| 10 | 56 | 136 | 111 | 27 | 24 | 23 | 72 | 144 | 60 |

SOURCE: Marks (1965)

We begin with an examination of the similarity among the 11 receptor cones. Each receptor cone is represented as a profile of light absorption across the nine colors of specified wavelengths. The first method that we present for accomplishing this task is a *principal components analysis* (PCA). As we shall see later, there are a variety of ways to measure the similarity among objects. In this case we use the Pearson correlation coefficient as the measure of similarity between all pairs of receptor cones. In general, the more similar the shape of the profiles of two cones across the colors, the higher the correlation between the two cones. Figure 1.1 presents a two-dimensional representation of the data derived from a principal components analysis of the correlations among receptor cones.

As expected, cones 11 and 10 are close together, as are cones 3 and 2. Note also that there are three fairly clear-cut clusters of points, with point number 7 somewhat of an outlier. For example, points 1, 2, and 3 form a very tight cluster in the upper-right part of the figure. This presents us with a visual representation of the fact that these points are very similar to each other as measured by correlations. Points 4, 5, and 6 also form a cluster, but not quite so tight as do 1, 2, and 3.

In order to illustrate the close connection between the visual representation and the correlations from which it is derived we might examine the correlations among points 4, 5, and 6. The correlations among points 4, 5, and 6 are as follows: $r_{4,5} = .85$, $r_{4,6} = .93$, and $r_{5,6} = .95$. Note that in the figure, points 5 and 6 are closest and have the highest

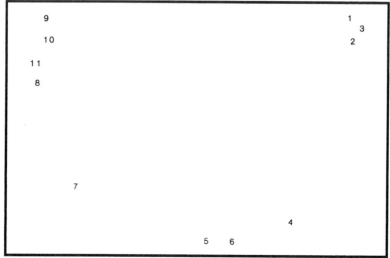

Figure 1.1. Principal Components Analysis of Receptor Cones

correlation. Points 4 and 5 are further apart and have a lower correlation. Such perfect correspondence is not always possible when representing large numbers of points in a small number of dimensions, however, the method attempts to produce as good a fit as possible.

Notice that PCA produces what looks like a reasonable picture of the cones but does not show us how the cones relate to color. We could have used PCA to give us a picture of the colors in terms of how similar they were to each other. That is, we can use the method to examine the cones or the colors separately but it does not show the joint relationship between them.

Another method, *multidimensional preference scaling* (MDPREF), allows us to see the joint relationship among the cones and colors. MDPREF was developed (Carroll, 1972; Carroll and Chang, 1970) for use with preference data. For example, a number of "judges" might rank their preferences for various flavors of ice cream (stimuli). The model represents the ice cream flavors in a spatial pattern according to their similarity across judges, and the judges' responses are fit into the configuration as vectors in such a way as to maximize the fit between the judges' choices and the ice cream configuration. If we let the receptor cones represent "judges" and a high absorption rate as indicat-

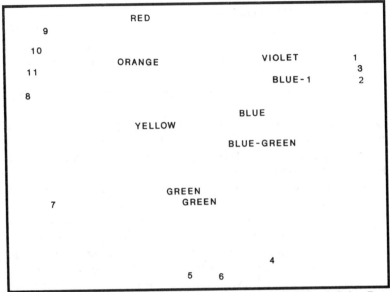

Figure 1.2. Multidimensional Preference Scaling (MDPREF) of Color Data
With Rows Standardized to Deviations From Means

ing "preference" for a color, we can apply the method to the data in Table 1.1.

Figure 1.2 is a graphic representation of MDPREF applied to the color data. Note that the receptor cones are almost in the same position here as they were in the principal component analysis. Here their relationship to the colors is displayed in the *same* figure. A vector drawn from each cone through the center of the figure represents the absorption rates. If we follow the vector from point 1 toward the center, we first encounter the colors Blue-1 and Violet. In Table 1.1 the absorption rates of cone 1 for Blue-1 and Violet are 153 and 147, respectively. Following the vector further we next come to Blue with an absorption rate of 89. Thus we find that each vector gives us a predicted ordering of color absorption for each cone.

The MDPREF representation has given us the same picture of the interrelationship among cones as did the principal component analysis. In addition it reveals, or graphically shows, the relationship between cones and colors. Note that the colors are in a continuous "horseshoe" shape ordering (note Figure 1.3 and chapter 7, p. 78). If one starts at

Violet and goes around the horseshoe, one gets the following ordering of colors given in wavelengths: 430, 458, 485, 498, 530, 540, 585, 610, and 660. The fact that the colors are ordered adds confirmation to the hypothesis that there is a consistent relation between the three kinds of receptor cones and the different wavelengths of color.

Another possible way of representing the relations among the receptor cones and the colors graphically is provided by *optimal scaling* or *correspondence analysis* (CA) used in an exploratory or descriptive mode. Inference, as we shall see, requires true frequency data in a contingency table format. This method also provides a way of representing both cones and colors in the same space. In this representation the similarities among cones or colors are on the same scale as the similarities between cones and colors.

Figure 1.3 shows the graphical results of such scaling of the color data. We have followed Schiffman and Falkenberg (1968: 199) in drawing a line connecting the colors in the order of their wavelengths to emphasize the relation between perceived colors and the wavelength spectrum. From this representation we can reproduce the predicted order of absorption of a given cone by drawing circles of increasing size around the point representing the cone. The degree of similarity in this representation is proportional to how close two points are located in the space. This "point" representation is distinct from the "vector" model of MDPREF. Correspondence analysis is also one way of implementing "unfolding" as introduced by Coombs (1964).

We would conclude from these analyses exactly what was reported by both Marks and Schiffman and Falkenberg, namely, that cones

1, 2, 3 are blue sensitive, 4, 5, 6 are green sensitive and 8, 9, 10, and 11 are red sensitive, while cone 7 is a double pigmented cone maximally sensitive in the green-orange. (Schiffman and Falkenberg, 1968: 199)

Working with much less information than was contained in Marks's original curves, and with the data randomized, the model orders the colors properly, places the cones correctly into three groups, and shows the relationship between the cones and the stimuli. (Schiffman and Falkenberg, 1968: 200)

It is important to note that the results of all three of these representations are consistent with one another. This should always be true, because the methods are very similar to each other in fundamental respects that will be discussed later in the monograph.

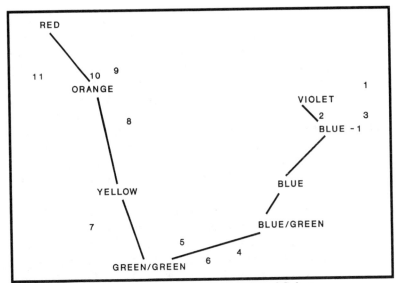

Figure 1.3. Correspondence Analysis with Ordering of Colors

These simple examples may provide a hint of the simplicity and exploratory power of these methods. We refer to these and other closely related methods as *metric scaling* methods. In later chapters we will show how these metric scaling techniques may all be calculated with the aid of *singular value decomposition*, which is simply a convenient method of revealing the basic structure of a matrix. Alternative methods include *nonmetric multidimensional scaling* (Kruskal and Wish, 1978) and *hierarchical clustering* (Aldenderfer and Blashfield, 1984; Arabie, Carroll, and DeSarbo, 1987; Mezzich and Solomon, 1980). We turn now to a consideration of the background of the main topic of the monograph, namely, metric scaling and its historical roots.

## Some Background Comments

Even if we limit our consideration to correspondence analysis or canonical analysis, as we do in the first part of these comments, we find an incredible amount of confusion in the literature. The confusion arises because different names are used for the same techniques by different people and in different fields. Also, it is not always realized that different computational procedures lead to the same results. The reasons for this are complex but probably the following factors have contributed the bulk of the difficulty. First, correspondence analysis or canonical analysis is so simple, fundamental, and far-reaching in its implications that it has been invented independently several times by researchers in different fields. Second, scholars in different fields tend not to read each other's work, so that developments in one field are not known by workers in different fields. Third, the major discoveries were made before the advent of computers so that the methods lay dormant waiting for implementation by modern computers. Fourth, because solutions are obtainable from a large number of different computational approaches, people using different computational approaches thought they were using different methods.

One author presents the following names for the same underlying procedure we call correspondence analysis (Nishisato, 1980: 11): the method of reciprocal averages, additive scoring, appropriate scoring, canonical analysis, Guttman weighting, principal components analysis of qualitative data, optimal scaling, Hayashi's theory of quantification, simultaneous linear regression, *analyse factorielle des correspondances*, correspondence factor analysis, correspondence analysis, biplot, and dual scaling. Despite a bewildering variety of different computational procedures used under these different labels it has been shown that all the methods share a fundamental mathematical structure (see especially Gittins, 1980; Greenacre, 1984; Nishisato, 1980). Tenenhaus and Young (1985) present a detailed derivation showing that the equations of multiple correspondence analysis are equivalent to four other approaches, namely, the method of reciprocal averages, analysis of variance, principal components analysis, and generalized canonical analysis. These five approaches, which were previously seen as disparate, are brought into a single statistical framework by their work.

Gittins (1980: 15-20) presents five different derivations of the method: singular value decomposition, eigenanalysis, least squares, the multivariate general linear model, and minimization of a Euclidean distance. Canonical analysis in its classical form is traced to two articles by Hotelling (1935, 1936) who uses Lagrange multipliers and eigenanalysis. Another contribution of Hotelling was the introduction of principal component analysis in 1933 (Hotelling, 1933). The psychological literature most frequently refers to "the Eckart-Young decomposition theorem", which traces to an early paper by Eckart and Young (1936) that clarified how a matrix could be decomposed into the row structure and the column structure. Eckart, we might note, was a physicist. Mathematicians and physicists had been aware for decades how to factor a matrix into its basic structure, but it was not until the 1930s that this knowledge diffused into the social science community. Thus, for example, even though Spearman (1904) had the idea of factor analysis in 1904 the computational implementation was not known until decades later.

The earliest paper that we have been able to find that contains a fully worked-out numerical example that corresponds exactly to current definitions is by Fisher (1940). We recalculated his data and were astounded to find that our results corresponded to the fifth decimal place with his results. Considering that computers were not invented until years after his work we find this a tribute to his computing skill. Guttman (1941) also published the method and it is important to note that Guttman and Fisher were unaware of each other's work.

The subsequent use and development of the methods involved the development of the computer and the contributions of countless researchers. That detailed history is best recounted in the sources referred to above. In order to give a unity to our own treatment we adopt singular value decomposition, which factors or decomposes a matrix into row and column structures together with the associated singular values, as a vehicle for the derivation and computation of metric scaling in a variety of forms. We find the presentation of metric scaling methods with singular value decomposition to be simpler and more intuitive than other methods. In addition it has great computational advantages over the other methods in terms of speed, accuracy, and generality. It should be noted that the singular value decomposition gives a least squares solution and that some advanced professionals prefer maximum likelihood solutions. These advanced methods are beyond the scope of this monograph but the solutions seldom differ in a way that affects interpretations (see Gilula and Haberman, 1986; Wasserman and Faust, 1989).

There is inevitably a great deal of ambiguity about terminology. We might note that the following sets of words all refer to the same concepts and may sometimes be used interchangeably in the following chapters. Row (or column) scores, optimal scores, factor loadings, factor scores, and coordinates are all rescalings of the row and column latent vectors or eigenvectors. The number of factors, dimensions, or components refer to the number of singular values and associated row and column vectors (appropriately rescaled) retained in the final representation.

**The Central Unifying Theme of the Monograph**

The central unifying theme of this monograph is that all metric scaling methods, including those not discussed in this monograph, may be seen as consisting of three parts or phases as follows: First, the original "data" are transformed by some normalization or transformation procedure. Second, a singular value decomposition of the transformed data summarizes the basic structure in the data with a set of row vectors, a set of column vectors, and a set of "singular values." Third, the sets of row and column vectors may be rescaled or otherwise weighted to provide a final set of row and column scores. Steps one and/or three may, in rare cases, be omitted. The second, crucial step of the singular value decomposition is always performed in metric scaling applications. In this monograph we describe and illustrate three forms of metric scaling. We indicate here how each of these methods is a variation on the central unifying theme. Detailed discussion will follow in latter chapters.

In PCA analysis the first step usually consists of computing a correlation matrix for either the row or the column variables. This has the effect of standardizing the rows or columns in the data. In the second step, decomposition results in summary vectors and the associated singular values. The third step may be omitted, although if we were plotting the results we might transform the vectors, for example, by weighting the vectors by the square root of the singular values.

In MDPREF the preprocessing generally consists of standardizing the rows in the original data matrix. The second step is the decomposition of the standardized matrix into singular values and row and column summary vectors. In the third step the row structure is rescaled and "superimposed" onto the configuration formed by the column summary vectors.

In correspondence analysis the data matrix is first transformed by dividing each cell in the matrix by the square root of the corresponding row and column totals. The transformed matrix is then decomposed with the singular value decomposition resulting in singular values (which in this case are canonical correlations) and a set of row vectors and column vectors. In the third stage the row and column vectors are rescaled with the original total frequencies to obtain "optimal scores." For plotting purposes the optimal scores are weighted by the square root of the singular values.

We might note that there are many scaling methods not covered in this monograph. They are all variations on our central unifying theme in one way or another. Some, like *individual differences scaling* or INDSCAL (Carroll and Chang, 1970), have generalized beyond the two-way decomposition to a three-way decomposition. Many other kinds of preprocessing have been tried in addition to the ones we have mentioned and each leads to a somewhat different set of scores. It is obvious from our statement of the central unifying theme that an understanding of the singular value decomposition is essential. We now turn to a description that provides insight into the basic structure of a matrix.

## 2. THE BASIC STRUCTURE
## OF A DATA MATRIX

A core operation in metric scaling is the decomposition of a matrix of data into its "basic structure." Such a decomposition represents the data as the product of three matrices with each matrix containing information regarding the underlying components of the original variables.

The process by which a matrix is decomposed into its basic structure is called *singular value decomposition* (SVD). For the purposes of this monograph we will treat SVD as a "black-box" operation, focusing on the interpretation and application of the component matrices and not on their derivation. Numeric algorithms and software are available to perform this procedure and we refer the reader to other sources for information on derivation and to applications packages (see Appendix). In this chapter we describe the basic structure of a data matrix and review the normalization procedures that will be used in subsequent chapters. It is assumed that the reader is familiar with introductory statistics and some of the simpler matrix algebra operations.

### Basic Structure of a Matrix

We begin with a description of the basic structure in data. We refer to the data set, the data *matrix*, as $X$ and to specific observations in $X$ as $x_{ij}$. The matrix may represent psychological test scores for a group of individuals, with each row in the data representing a unique subject and each column representing a particular test. Each cell in the matrix,

$x_{ij}$, would contain subject $i$'s score for test $j$. The matrix could also be a form of contingency table where cell values represent actual frequencies of the corresponding, cross-classified row and column variables. For example, the row variables may be cities, the columns may be types of crimes, and the cell values would indicate the number of each type of crime occurring in each city.

Any data matrix can be decomposed into its "characteristic" components. For a matrix with $n$ rows and $m$ columns, where $n > m$, the basic structure information is contained in three matrices, as illustrated in Example 2.1.

The $\mathbf{U}$ matrix "summarizes" the information in the rows of $\mathbf{X}$. Rows in $\mathbf{U}$ correspond to the rows in $\mathbf{X}$ and the columns in $\mathbf{U}$ represent the underlying dimensions or components in the row variables. Similarly, the $\mathbf{V}$ matrix summarizes information in the columns of $\mathbf{X}$. Rows in $\mathbf{V}$ correspond to columns in $\mathbf{X}$ and the columns in $\mathbf{V}$ summarize the underlying components in the columns in $\mathbf{X}$. The number of rows in $\mathbf{U}$ equals the number of rows in $\mathbf{X}$ and the number of rows in $\mathbf{V}$ equals the number of columns in $\mathbf{X}$. The columns in the $\mathbf{U}$ and $\mathbf{V}$ matrices represent the underlying dimensions or basic *components* in the structure of the data.

The $\mathbf{d}$ matrix is a special kind of matrix, a *diagonal matrix*, that is square and all off-diagonal entries are zeros. The diagonal entries in $\mathbf{d}$ contain the *singular values* corresponding to the columns of the $\mathbf{U}$ and $\mathbf{V}$ matrices. The first entry, $d_{11}$, corresponds to the first column of $\mathbf{U}$ *and* to the first column of $\mathbf{V}$; the second entry, $d_{22}$, corresponds to the second column of $\mathbf{U}$ and the second column of $\mathbf{V}$. The values in $\mathbf{d}$ are "weights" indicating the relative "importance" of each dimension in $\mathbf{U}$ and $\mathbf{V}$ and are ordered from largest to smallest. The columns of $\mathbf{U}$ and $\mathbf{V}$ and the elements of $\mathbf{d}$ are ordered from most to least "important" in the overall structure of $\mathbf{X}$. If $\mathbf{X}$ does not contain redundant information, the number of columns in $\mathbf{U}$ and $\mathbf{V}$, and the dimensions of $\mathbf{d}$ will equal the minimum dimension $m$ of $\mathbf{X}$.

Example 2.2 shows a numeric example with a $5 \times 3$ matrix. The basic structure of $\mathbf{X}$ is represented in the $\mathbf{U}$, $\mathbf{d}$, and $\mathbf{V}$ matrices. In fact, $\mathbf{X}$ is the product of the $\mathbf{U}$, $\mathbf{d}$, and $\mathbf{V}^T$ matrices. Note that the transpose of $\mathbf{V}$ ($\mathbf{V}^T$) is used to multiply the matrices together.

$$\mathbf{X}_{(n \times m)} = \mathbf{U}_{(n \times m)}\, \mathbf{d}_{(m \times m)}\, \mathbf{V}^T_{(m \times m)} = \mathbf{U}\mathbf{d}\mathbf{V}^T_{(n \times m)}$$

The basic structure of a matrix is like the layers of an onion; the components can be peeled off, one by one, and reassembled partially,

EXAMPLE 2.1

Notation for Basic Structure

$$
\begin{bmatrix}
x_{11} & x_{12} & \cdots & x_{1m} \\
x_{21} & x_{22} & \cdots & x_{2m} \\
\cdot & & & \\
\cdot & & & \\
\cdot & & & \\
x_{n1} & x_{n2} & \cdots & x_{nm}
\end{bmatrix}
\rightarrow
\begin{bmatrix}
U_{11} & U_{12} & \cdots & U_{1m} \\
U_{21} & U_{22} & \cdots & U_{2m} \\
\cdot & & & \\
\cdot & & & \\
\cdot & & & \\
U_{n1} & U_{n2} & \cdots & U_{nm}
\end{bmatrix}
\begin{bmatrix}
d_{11} & 0 & \cdots & 0 \\
0 & d_{22} & \cdots & 0 \\
\cdot & & & \\
\cdot & & & \\
0 & 0 & \cdots & d_{mm}
\end{bmatrix}
\begin{bmatrix}
V_{11} & V_{12} & \cdots & V_{1m} \\
V_{21} & V_{22} & \cdots & V_{2m} \\
\cdot & & & \\
\cdot & & & \\
V_{m1} & V_{m2} & \cdots & V_{mm}
\end{bmatrix}
$$

$$\mathbf{X}_{(n \times m)} \qquad \mathbf{U}_{(n \times m)} \qquad \mathbf{d}_{(m \times m)} \qquad \mathbf{V}_{(m \times m)}$$

or in whole. A one-dimensional estimate of $\mathbf{X}$ can be obtained by multiplying together the first column vector in $\mathbf{U}$, the first element in $\mathbf{d}$, and the first column vector in $\mathbf{V}$ (i.e., the first row of $\mathbf{V}^T$). A two-dimensional estimate can be obtained by multiplying the first two $\mathbf{U}$ column vectors, the first two diagonal elements in $\mathbf{d}$, and the first two $\mathbf{V}$ column vectors. A three-dimensional estimate of $\mathbf{X}$ can be obtained by using all three $\mathbf{U}$ column vectors, all three $d_{ii}$'s, and all three $\mathbf{V}$ column vectors.

This successive approximation of $\mathbf{X}$, from Example 2.2, is illustrated in Example 2.3. A one-dimensional estimate of $\mathbf{X}$ is illustrated in the first horizontal set of matrices. The second set estimates $\mathbf{X}$ from only the second component vectors. The bottom set of matrices provides a two-dimensional estimate of $\mathbf{X}$. Note that the estimate of $\mathbf{X}$ from first component $(U_{i1}, d_{11}, V_{1j}^T)$ and the estimate from the second component $(U_{i2}, d_{22}, V_{2j}^T)$ could have been added together, cell by cell, to obtain the two-dimensional estimate at the bottom. Similarly, one-, two- and three-dimensional estimates can be obtained.

If $\mathbf{X}$ contains redundant information, it is summarized in the $\mathbf{U}$, $\mathbf{d}$, and $\mathbf{V}$ matrices. In Example 2.4, three additional columns have been included in the data matrix from Example 2.2: The fourth column is an exact duplicate of the first, the fifth column is equal to the second column times two, and the sixth column is the sum of the second and third columns. In other words, the new matrix contains no new information; and the data in the new columns are completely redundant with the first three columns. Note that in $\mathbf{V}$ the first and fourth rows are identical; the coordinates for the fifth row are equal to those for the second row times two; and the coordinates for the sixth row equal the sum of the coordinates for the second and third rows. Thus the maximum

## EXAMPLE 2.2

### An Example of Basic Structure

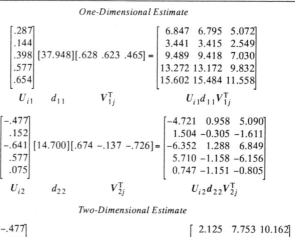

$$
\begin{bmatrix} 2 & 8 & 10 \\ 5 & 3 & 1 \\ 4 & 9 & 15 \\ 20 & 10 & 5 \\ 15 & 18 & 9 \end{bmatrix} \rightarrow \begin{bmatrix} .287 & -.477 & -.066 \\ .144 & .152 & .029 \\ .398 & -.641 & .454 \\ .557 & .577 & .535 \\ .654 & .075 & -.709 \end{bmatrix} \begin{bmatrix} 37.948 & 0 & 0 \\ 0 & 14.700 & 0 \\ 0 & 0 & 4.888 \end{bmatrix} \begin{bmatrix} .628 & .674 & .389 \\ .623 & -.137 & -.770 \\ .465 & -.726 & .506 \end{bmatrix}
$$

|    X    |    U    |    d    |    V    |

## EXAMPLE 2.3

### Estimation of Data with Reduced Dimensionality

*One-Dimensional Estimate*

$$
\begin{bmatrix} .287 \\ .144 \\ .398 \\ .577 \\ .654 \end{bmatrix} [37.948][.628\ .623\ .465] = \begin{bmatrix} 6.847 & 6.795 & 5.072 \\ 3.441 & 3.415 & 2.549 \\ 9.489 & 9.418 & 7.030 \\ 13.272 & 13.172 & 9.832 \\ 15.602 & 15.484 & 11.558 \end{bmatrix}
$$

$$
U_{i1} \qquad d_{11} \qquad V_{1j}^T \qquad\qquad U_{i1}d_{11}V_{1j}^T
$$

$$
\begin{bmatrix} -.477 \\ .152 \\ -.641 \\ .577 \\ .075 \end{bmatrix} [14.700][.674\ -.137\ -.726] = \begin{bmatrix} -4.721 & 0.958 & 5.090 \\ 1.504 & -0.305 & -1.611 \\ -6.352 & 1.288 & 6.849 \\ 5.710 & -1.158 & -6.156 \\ 0.747 & -1.151 & -0.805 \end{bmatrix}
$$

$$
U_{i2} \qquad d_{22} \qquad V_{2j}^T \qquad\qquad U_{i2}d_{22}V_{2j}^T
$$

*Two-Dimensional Estimate*

$$
\begin{bmatrix} .287 & -.477 \\ .144 & .152 \\ .398 & -.641 \\ .557 & .577 \\ .654 & .075 \end{bmatrix} \begin{bmatrix} 37.948 & 0 \\ 0 & 14.700 \end{bmatrix} \begin{bmatrix} .628 & .623 & .465 \\ .674 & -.137 & -.726 \end{bmatrix} = \begin{bmatrix} 2.125 & 7.753 & 10.162 \\ 4.944 & 3.110 & 0.928 \\ 3.137 & 10.707 & 13.879 \\ 18.982 & 12.014 & 3.676 \\ 16.349 & 15.333 & 10.753 \end{bmatrix}
$$

$$
U_2 \qquad\qquad d_2 \qquad\qquad V_2^T \qquad\qquad U_2 d_2 V_2^T
$$

meaningful dimension of **X** is three. This maximum dimension is also called the *rank* of matrix **X**.

Rank is the dimension of the subspace spanned by the configuration of data points. It is equal to the number of nonzero elements in the **d** matrix. In Example 2.4, each row in **X** can be considered as a point plotted in six-dimensional space. The number of elements in the **d** matrix, however, indicates that this configuration could be plotted in

EXAMPLE 2.4

Basic Structure with Reduced Rank

$$
\begin{bmatrix} 2 & 8 & 10 & 2 & 16 & 18 \\ 5 & 3 & 1 & 5 & 6 & 4 \\ 4 & 9 & 15 & 4 & 18 & 24 \\ 20 & 10 & 5 & 20 & 20 & 15 \\ 15 & 18 & 9 & 15 & 36 & 27 \end{bmatrix} \rightarrow
\begin{bmatrix} .331 & .452 & .006 \\ .129 & -.166 & -.023 \\ .423 & .561 & -.531 \\ .470 & -.669 & -.510 \\ .688 & -.074 & .676 \end{bmatrix}
\begin{bmatrix} 77.585 & 0 & 0 \\ 0 & 21.273 & 0 \\ 0 & 0 & 7.748 \end{bmatrix}
\begin{bmatrix} .293 & -.572 & -.294 \\ .308 & .007 & .294 \\ .236 & .412 & -.566 \\ .293 & -.572 & -.294 \\ .617 & .013 & .589 \\ .545 & .418 & -.272 \end{bmatrix}
$$

| $\mathbf{X}_{(5 \times 6)}$ | $\mathbf{U}_{(5 \times 3)}$ | $\mathbf{d}_{(3 \times 3)}$ | $\mathbf{V}_{(6 \times 3)}$ |
|---|---|---|---|

three dimensions *with no loss of information*. A configuration can be represented in a dimensionality equal to its rank, $k$:

$$\mathbf{X}_{(n \times m)} = \mathbf{U}_{(n \times k)}\, \mathbf{d}_{(k \times k)}\, \mathbf{V}^{T}_{(m \times k)}$$

Thus the row variables can be described with three *dimensions* instead of the original six.

Spatially, the basic structure matrices re-represent or "rotate" the data points in $\mathbf{X}$ in $n$-dimensional Euclidean space. The $\mathbf{U}$, $\mathbf{d}$, and $\mathbf{V}$ matrices "relocate" the data points onto new coordinate vectors. The original configuration of data points may be rotated, stretched or shrunk, and possibly reflected (mirror image). The row variables of $\mathbf{X}$ then become points on the $\mathbf{U}$ column coordinates, and the column variables of $\mathbf{X}$ become points on the $\mathbf{V}$ column coordinates. The coordinate vectors are perpendicular or *orthogonal* to each other and are normalized to unit length:

$$1.0 = \left( \sum_i U_{ik}^2 \right)^{1/2} = \left( \sum_j V_{jk}^2 \right)^{1/2}$$

The columns within $\mathbf{U}$ and the columns within $\mathbf{V}$ are said to be *orthonormal*.

Thus "component" or column vectors in $\mathbf{U}$ and $\mathbf{V}$ are coordinates for representing the data points in a normalized, spatial configuration with possible reduced dimensionality. The $\mathbf{d}$ values, the singular values, are "weights" that correspond to the columns of $\mathbf{U}$ and $\mathbf{V}$ and may be used to "stretch" the vectors. Stretching the configuration *un*normalizes it, returning it to its original "shape." For example, a football-shaped cluster of points would look more like a round ball in a normalized, that is, orthonormal configuration. Multiplication of the coordinate values in $\mathbf{U}$ or $\mathbf{V}$ by their $\mathbf{d}$'s would restore the football-like shape.

If a matrix is symmetric, then the resulting row and column component matrices will be equal. The basic structure of a symmetric matrix **S** is:

$$\mathbf{S} = \mathbf{U}\mathbf{d}\mathbf{V}^{\mathrm{T}} = \mathbf{U}\mathbf{d}\mathbf{U}^{\mathrm{T}} = \mathbf{V}\mathbf{d}\mathbf{V}^{\mathrm{T}}$$

Pre- or postmultiplication of a matrix by its transpose ($\mathbf{X}^{\mathrm{T}}\mathbf{X}$ or $\mathbf{X}\mathbf{X}^{\mathrm{T}}$) results in a square, symmetric matrix. Decomposition of **X**, $\mathbf{X}\mathbf{X}^{\mathrm{T}}$, or $\mathbf{X}^{\mathrm{T}}\mathbf{X}$ reveals "the same" basic structure.

$$\mathbf{X} = \mathbf{U}\mathbf{d}\mathbf{V}^{\mathrm{T}}$$

$$\mathbf{X}\mathbf{X}^{\mathrm{T}} = \mathbf{U}\mathbf{d}^{2}\mathbf{U}^{\mathrm{T}}$$

$$\mathbf{X}^{\mathrm{T}}\mathbf{X} = \mathbf{V}\mathbf{d}^{2}\mathbf{V}^{\mathrm{T}}$$

Further, $\mathrm{rank}(\mathbf{X}) = \mathrm{rank}(\mathbf{X}^{\mathrm{T}}) = \mathrm{rank}(\mathbf{X}\mathbf{X}^{\mathrm{T}}) = \mathrm{rank}(\mathbf{X}^{\mathrm{T}}\mathbf{X})$.

The basic structure of a square, symmetric matrix is equivalent to its *eigenstructure* (*eigen* is German for characteristic). In this special case, the decomposition of a symmetric matrix, the component column vectors of **U** or **V** may be referred to as *eigenvectors* or *characteristic vectors*. The diagonal values of **d**, the singular values, may be referred to as *eigenvalues, characteristic roots*, or *latent roots*. Another special case occurs in the decomposition of a symmetric matrix in that the sum of the eigenvalues or singular values is equal to the sum of the main diagonal entries of **X** (the *trace* of the matrix). Of interest is the fact that the basic structure of a rectangular (nonsquare, nonsymmetric) matrix may be solved by performing eigenanalyses, even though a rectangular matrix does not have an eigenstructure. A rectangular matrix, **X**, can be made into two symmetric matrices ($\mathbf{X}\mathbf{X}^{\mathrm{T}}$, $\mathbf{X}^{\mathrm{T}}\mathbf{X}$) and their eigenstructures can be used to obtain the basic structure of **X**. If $\mathbf{X}\mathbf{X}^{\mathrm{T}} = \mathbf{U}\mathbf{D}\mathbf{U}^{\mathrm{T}}$ and $\mathbf{X}^{\mathrm{T}}\mathbf{X} = \mathbf{V}\mathbf{D}\mathbf{V}^{\mathrm{T}}$ then $\mathbf{X} = \mathbf{U}\mathbf{D}^{1/2}\mathbf{V}^{\mathrm{T}}$. Thus

> the singular-value decomposition of the matrix **X**, . . . provides information that encompasses that given by the eigensystem of $\mathbf{X}^{\mathrm{T}}\mathbf{X}$. As a practical matter, however, there are reasons for preferring the use of the singular-value decomposition. First, it applies directly to the data matrix **X** that is the focus of our concern, and not to the cross-product matrix $\mathbf{X}^{\mathrm{T}}\mathbf{X}$. . . . And . . . whereas the eigensystem and the SVD of a given matrix are mathematically equivalent, computationally they are not. Algorithms exist that allow the singular-value decomposition of **X** to be computed with greater numerical stability than is possible in computing the eigensystem of $\mathbf{X}^{\mathrm{T}}\mathbf{X}$, particularly in the case where the rank of **X** is less than the dimensions of **X**. (Belsley, Kuh, and Welsch, 1980: 99)

**Transformations**

Principal components analysis (PCA), multidimensional preference scaling (MDPREF), and correspondence analysis (CA) all involve finding the basic structure in a data matrix. They share a common decomposition algorithm, that is, SVD, and differ only in their predecomposition transformations of the data and their postdecomposition transformations of the component latent vectors. Explicitly or implicitly these methods may transform the data during or prior to analysis. For example, PCA of a covariance or correlation matrix implicitly involves a correction for means or standardization, respectively. MDPREF may be preceded by a correction for means, standardization, or double-centering of the data. In CA each value is divided by the geometric mean of the corresponding marginal totals. Because transformations are the main difference between these methods, we review several possible transformations in this section.

Transformations may be performed within row *or* within column variables, within rows *and* columns, or pairwise patterns among row variables *or* among column variables can be calculated. Probably the most familiar type of normalization is standardization. To standardize a variable, it is transformed via a linear transformation so that the mean becomes zero and the standard deviation one. Because addition or subtraction of a constant affects only the mean of a variable, each variable can be transformed so that the new mean is zero by reexpressing each value as a *deviation from the mean*:

$$x_{ij}^* = x_{ij} - \overline{X}_i \qquad [2.1]$$

Multiplication or division by a constant affects both the mean and the standard deviation, so that if the variable $X$ is multiplied by the inverse of its standard deviation $(1/\sigma_X)$ the new standard deviation becomes one. Thus the linear transformation for *standardization* is:

$$x_{ij}^* = \frac{x_{ij} - \overline{X}_j}{\sigma_i} \qquad [2.2]$$

A variable also may be transformed so that it is of unit length when projected in space. This transformation is similar to standardization in that variables are reexpressed on a common scale. Spatially, the end points of unit length vectors (the stimulus points) appear on the surface of an *n*-dimensional sphere; and in two dimensions they form an arc. To transform or normalize a variable to *unit length*:

$$x_{ij}^* = x_{ij} \bigg/ \left( \sum_i x_{ij}^2 \right)^{1/2} \qquad [2.3]$$

Standardization and unit norming differ only by a constant: A standardized variable divided by the square root of the number of observations ($n$ if descriptive standard deviation is used and $n - 1$ if the inferential formula is used) becomes a unit length vector; and if elements in a unit length vector are multiplied by the square root of the number of observations ($n$ or $n - 1$) they become standardized.

A common transformation for categorical or frequency data is to divide category sums by the total number of observations. In a table of cross-classified data the original entry may be changed into a *proportion* (or *percentage*):

$$x_{ij}^* = x_{ij} \bigg/ \sum_i x_{ij} \qquad \text{or} \qquad x_{ij}^* = x_{ij} \bigg/ \sum_j x_{ij} \qquad [2.4]$$

The "simplest" transformation is a "reflection." For example, data that have been collected where $1$ = most to $k$ = least can be transformed by multiplying all values by $-1$ or by subtracting the data from a constant $(k + 1)$. This transformation reverses the ordering so that the largest number indicates "most" and smallest number the "least."

Sometimes it is desirable to transform both row *and* column variables. This can be done simultaneously or iteratively. Row or column variables may be transformed into deviates from their respective means using equation 2.1. The removal of both row and column means can be performed in two steps or in one step with *double-centering*. Double-centering removes only mean effects, leaving differences in variances unchanged:

$$x_{ij}^* = x_{ij} - \overline{X}_i - \overline{X}_j + \overline{\overline{X}}_{ij} \qquad [2.5]$$

Both standardization (equation 2.2) and a proportional transformation (equation 2.4) can be performed iteratively. Standardization of rows and columns of a data matrix can be repeated until row and column means are zero and within-row and within-column standard deviations are one. A proportional transformation of rows and columns performed iteratively is called *iterative proportional fitting*. It can be used to remove differences in row and column totals by iterating to "equal" sizes, leaving the pattern of association within the table unaffected (Dixon, Brown, et al., 1979: 270; Mosteller, 1968). Iterative proportional fitting is used most commonly in the log-linear models to find the expected values (Bishop, Fienberg, and Holland, 1975; Fienberg, 1980).

A transformation with a similar effect removes differences in marginal totals and expresses each cell as a proportion. This "square root" transformation divides each cell by the geometric mean of the corresponding marginal totals:

$$x_{ij}^* = x_{ij} \Big/ \left( \sum_i x_{ij} \sum_j x_{ij} \right)^{1/2} = x_{ij}/(x_i.x._j)^{1/2} \qquad [2.6]$$

Some "transformations" reexpress data as pairwise measures of similarity in "pattern." These transformations are usually the result of cross-product multiplication. In matrix notion, the cross-product matrix is a matrix times its transpose: $\mathbf{XX}^T$ is the cross-product matrix for row variables in $\mathbf{X}$, and $\mathbf{X}^T\mathbf{X}$ is the cross-product matrix for the column variables.

A covariance matrix can be obtained from a cross-product matrix of mean-corrected data. If the original data have been corrected for column means, then a cross-product matrix can be obtained:

$$\mathbf{B} = \mathbf{X}_d^T \mathbf{X}_d \qquad [2.7]$$

The *covariance matrix* for column variables may be found by dividing that cross-product matrix by the number of row observations

$$\mathbf{C} = \frac{1}{n}\mathbf{B} = \frac{1}{n}\mathbf{X}_d^T\mathbf{X}_d \qquad [2.8]$$

creating a covariance matrix among the column variables of $\mathbf{X}$. A covariance matrix can be calculated for the rows of $\mathbf{X}$ by first correcting $\mathbf{X}$ for row means, then

$$\mathbf{C} = \frac{1}{m}\mathbf{X}_d\mathbf{X}_d^T \qquad [2.9]$$

where $m$ is the number of columns in $\mathbf{X}$.

By correcting covariances ($c_{ij}$) for scale differences of each variable, a pure pattern measure is obtained. The Pearson correlation coefficient, $r$ is:

$$r_{ij} = c_{ij} / \sigma_i \sigma_j$$

If the columns in $\mathbf{X}$ are standardized, a correlation matrix can be calculated in the form of a cross-product matrix:

$$\mathbf{R} = \tfrac{1}{n}\mathbf{X}_s^T\mathbf{X}_s = \tfrac{1}{n}\mathbf{Z}_c^T\mathbf{Z}_c \qquad [2.10]$$

where $\mathbf{X}_s$ ($\mathbf{Z}_c$) is a matrix standardized within *columns*, $n$ is the number of row observations in $\mathbf{X}$, and $\mathbf{R}$ is a matrix containing correlation coefficients among all pairs of $m$ columns in $\mathbf{X}$. Similarly, a matrix $\mathbf{Q}$ can be obtained for the correlations among the rows of $\mathbf{X}$:

$$\mathbf{Q} = \tfrac{1}{m}\mathbf{X}_s\mathbf{X}_s^T = \tfrac{1}{m}\mathbf{Z}_r\mathbf{Z}_r^T \qquad [2.11]$$

where $\mathbf{X}_s$ ($\mathbf{Z}_r$) indicates the matrix $\mathbf{X}$ standardized within *rows*, and $m$ is the number of column variables. If standardization is performed with the inferential formula for the standard deviation ($n-1$ in the denominator), then the correction factors $1/n$ and $1/m$ in equations 2.10 and 2.11 become $1/(n-1)$ and $1/(m-1)$. Note that just as a covariance matrix implicitly incorporates a correction for means, standardization is always implicit in the calculation of a correlation coefficient.

In this chapter we saw that the basic structure in a data matrix $\mathbf{X}$ can be represented as the product of three matrices (Example 2.1) and that the basic structure of that data is not affected by cross-product multiplication ($\mathbf{X}^T\mathbf{X}$, $\mathbf{X}\mathbf{X}^T$). Data normalization and standardization transformations, however, can affect the basic structure. Such transformations performed prior to factorization affect the basic structure, because the basic structure represents the *transformed* data ($\mathbf{X}^*$) and not the original observations ($\mathbf{X}$).

# 3. PRINCIPAL COMPONENTS ANALYSIS

In this chapter we describe principal components analysis. Principal components analysis (PCA) is probably one of the best known metric scaling procedures. With PCA, a large set of variables may be reduced to a smaller set of summary variables based on the pattern of statistical similarity among the original variables (Chatfield and Collins, 1980; Dunteman, 1989).

Mathematically, PCA finds the basic structure of a data matrix via a cross-product matrix. Typically, standardized data are used, although mean-corrected data or the original "raw" data can be used. These three data "types" correspond to implicit transformations made prior to the calculation of a cross-product matrix: correlation, covariance, or a "raw" cross-product matrix. Here, we assume that the standardized data are being used (correlation matrix), although the discussion can be extended to other transformations. In this chapter, we describe PCA in terms of factoring a cross-product matrix (e.g., a correlation matrix) and in terms of the basic structure of the *data*.

## Single Factor Example

To illustrate how a set of variables can be summarized with PCA, we use a simulated example based on socioeconomic data collected in rural Guatemala. We assume that there exists an underlying ordering of households in terms of financial resources and that the true score of each household is not directly measurable. Information can be collected on variables potentially related to financial resources, such as the number of chickens, the number of rooms in the house, number of appliances, monthly income, amount of land owned, the number of bicycles, and the number of income-earning household members; and PCA can be used to combine the variables into a single index of financial resources.

In the construction of an index, each of the proxy variables is assumed to be associated with the underlying and unknown degree of financial resources. If this is true, the variables also will be positively correlated with one another (Nunnally, 1978). Simulated responses from 20 households were obtained for seven variables using a common elements method (Snedecor and Cochran, 1972: 181; Weller, 1987). An interval scale ordering for the 20 households was generated and hypo-thetical responses to seven variables created so that the average corre-lation between the variables and the "true score" would be between .60 and 1.00 (.80 on average) and the average intercorrelation among the seven variables would be .64. The simulated data, standardized by columns, appear in Table 3.1. The interval-scaled "true" financial re-sources score for each household is in the last column of Table 3.1.

To summarize these variables mathematically, we find the basic structure in the data. We can obtain the basic structure directly with an SVD, or indirectly by factoring a cross-product matrix. The basic structure of the column standardized data $(\mathbf{Z}_c)$ is

$$\mathbf{Z}_c = \mathbf{U}\mathbf{d}\mathbf{V}^T$$

and appears down the left-hand side of Table 3.2. PCA factors a square, symmetric cross-product matrix, in this case a correlation matrix $(\mathbf{R})$ calculated among the seven financial resource variables:

TABLE 3.1

Standardized Financial Resources Data

| Case | Chickens | Rooms | Appliances | Income | Land | Bicycles | Earners | True Score |
|------|----------|-------|------------|--------|------|----------|---------|------------|
| a | -0.798 | -0.834 | -0.089 | -0.908 | -0.630 | -1.684 | 0.120 | 1963 |
| b | 0.511 | 0.245 | -0.652 | -0.303 | 0.748 | 0.667 | 0.374 | 2137 |
| c | 0.476 | 0.305 | 1.038 | 1.726 | 0.961 | 1.345 | 1.322 | 2338 |
| d | -1.025 | -0.509 | -1.513 | -0.611 | -0.697 | -0.752 | -0.827 | 1900 |
| e | -0.495 | 0.046 | 0.654 | 0.800 | 0.159 | 1.465 | -0.158 | 2072 |
| f | 1.034 | 0.227 | 1.056 | 1.097 | 0.438 | 0.667 | 0.696 | 2221 |
| g | 0.297 | -0.611 | 0.134 | -0.211 | 0.305 | -0.145 | 0.114 | 2094 |
| h | -0.984 | -1.256 | -1.568 | -1.371 | -1.347 | -0.752 | -0.976 | 1843 |
| i | -0.784 | 0.636 | -0.918 | -0.411 | -0.084 | 0.413 | 1.167 | 2133 |
| j | 0.779 | 0.986 | 0.815 | 0.789 | 0.912 | -1.712 | 1.415 | 2214 |
| k | -0.736 | -0.177 | -0.572 | -0.520 | -0.491 | 0.243 | -0.449 | 1965 |
| l | -1.948 | -1.822 | -0.436 | -0.651 | -1.602 | -0.173 | -1.087 | 1822 |
| m | 1.448 | 1.823 | 0.487 | 0.526 | 1.586 | 1.465 | 1.099 | 2354 |
| n | -0.013 | 0.431 | -0.683 | -1.348 | -1.298 | -0.604 | -1.725 | 1938 |
| o | 0.394 | -0.346 | -0.336 | -0.160 | -0.485 | -0.442 | -0.406 | 1992 |
| p | 1.138 | 0.654 | 0.883 | 1.326 | 1.106 | 1.034 | 0.486 | 2276 |
| q | -1.266 | -1.840 | -1.822 | -0.463 | -1.007 | -0.886 | -0.102 | 1856 |
| r | 1.406 | 0.787 | 0.951 | -0.634 | 1.112 | 0.469 | -0.257 | 2278 |
| s | -0.612 | -0.448 | 1.403 | -0.766 | -1.049 | -1.310 | -2.016 | 1933 |
| t | 1.179 | 1.703 | 1.168 | 2.097 | 1.361 | 0.695 | 1.210 | 2267 |

$$\mathbf{R} = \frac{1}{n-1} \mathbf{Z}_c^T \mathbf{Z}_c = \mathbf{V} \mathbf{D} \mathbf{V}^T$$

where $\mathbf{V}$ is the set of characteristic vectors for the financial variables, and $\mathbf{D}$ is the set of singular values associated with each column vector in $\mathbf{V}$. Because the basic structure of a square, symmetric matrix is equivalent to the eigenstructure, the component or characteristic column vectors in $\mathbf{V}$ are oftentimes called *eigenvectors* and the singular values in $\mathbf{D}$ are called *characteristic roots* or *eigenvalues*. The eigenvectors or principal components for the financial resource variables appear in the top left ($\mathbf{V}$ matrix) of Table 3.2. The corresponding eigenvalues appear in the right-hand, middle panel of Table 3.2. Note that the eigenvalues can be obtained with PCA or by transforming the basic structure singular values [$\mathbf{D} = \mathbf{d}^2/(n-1)$].

Although we began with seven variables, we find that they can be well represented by a single principal component. This is evident, first, in the pattern of eigenvalues. Recall that the sum of the main diagonal elements of a square, symmetric matrix equals the sum of its eigenvalues. Because the main diagonal elements in a covariance or correla-

TABLE 3.2

## Basic Structure and PCA Results for Column-Standardized Financial Variables

**V Matrix**

| | Fac1 | Fac2 | Fac3 | Fac4 | V Matrix Factor Loadings | Fac1 | Fac2 | Fac3 | Fac4 |
|---|---|---|---|---|---|---|---|---|---|
| Chickens | .402 | −.326 | −.116 | −.333 | Chickens | .876 | −.287 | −.089 | −.244 |
| Rooms | .394 | −.209 | −.128 | −.467 | Rooms | .858 | −.184 | −.098 | −.342 |
| Appliances | .334 | −.596 | .286 | .476 | Appliances | .727 | −.524 | .220 | .349 |
| Income | .393 | .195 | .077 | .571 | Income | .855 | .171 | .060 | .419 |
| Land | .442 | .042 | −.153 | −.125 | Land | .963 | .037 | −.118 | −.092 |
| Bicycles | .308 | .475 | .752 | −.256 | Bicycles | .651 | .417 | .580 | −.188 |
| Earners | .356 | .480 | −.542 | .193 | Earners | .776 | .422 | −.417 | .142 |
| Singular Values | 9.491 | 3.835 | 3.359 | 3.199 | Eigenvalues | 4.741 | .774 | .594 | .539 |

Proportion of Explained Variance

| | | | | | | .667 | .111 | .085 | .077 |
|---|---|---|---|---|---|---|---|---|---|

**U Matrix**

| | Fac1 | Fac2 | Fac3 | Fac4 | U Matrix Factor Scores | Fac1 | Fac2 | Fac3 | Fac4 |
|---|---|---|---|---|---|---|---|---|---|
| a | −.189 | −.119 | −.337 | .196 | a | −.822 | −.520 | −1.470 | .854 |
| b | .067 | .167 | −.034 | −.300 | b | .292 | .726 | −.150 | −1.308 |
| c | .279 | .212 | .144 | .303 | c | 1.215 | .923 | .629 | 1.322 |
| d | −.231 | .115 | −.091 | −.116 | d | −1.007 | .500 | −.399 | −.505 |
| e | .086 | .142 | .436 | .152 | e | .375 | .619 | 1.899 | .662 |
| f | .204 | −.034 | .088 | .184 | f | .889 | −.149 | .384 | .801 |
| g | −.003 | −.024 | −.045 | .047 | g | −.013 | −.104 | −.197 | .205 |
| h | −.330 | .096 | −.033 | −.139 | h | −1.436 | .419 | −.144 | −.604 |
| i | −.003 | .350 | −.177 | −.180 | i | −.012 | 1.526 | −.770 | −.786 |
| j | .175 | −.231 | −.630 | .224 | j | .764 | −1.008 | −2.746 | .977 |
| k | −.112 | .103 | .121 | −.103 | k | −.488 | .450 | .526 | −.449 |
| l | −.322 | .125 | .294 | .298 | l | −1.402 | .543 | 1.280 | 1.299 |
| m | .339 | .065 | .013 | −.363 | m | 1.476 | .282 | .057 | −1.582 |
| n | −.207 | −.290 | .097 | −.409 | n | −.904 | −1.262 | .422 | −1.783 |
| o | −.068 | −.081 | −.044 | −.039 | o | −.298 | −.355 | −.192 | −.171 |
| p | .265 | −.001 | .144 | .058 | p | 1.153 | −.006 | .629 | .251 |
| q | −.293 | .334 | −.188 | .150 | q | −1.276 | 1.456 | −.821 | .656 |
| r | .157 | −.304 | .084 | −.329 | r | .684 | −1.327 | .365 | −1.436 |
| s | −.194 | −.606 | .219 | .225 | s | −.846 | −2.643 | .955 | .981 |
| t | .380 | −.016 | −.059 | .141 | t | 1.656 | −.068 | −.258 | .616 |

tion matrix are variances (in a correlation matrix the variables are standardized), the ratio of an eigenvalue or a cumulative sum of eigenvalues over the total sum (the trace of the matrix) is often described as "explained variance." In this example, the sum of the main diagonal elements of the correlation matrix equals seven, the number of variables equals seven, and the sum of the eigenvalues equals seven. The first principal component or factor "accounts for" 4.741/7.000 or 67.7% of the "total variance" and the second factor for 11.1% of the total. The precipitous drop in size of adjacent eigenvalues indicates that this is a single factor structure. In this case, the "variance" represented on the second through seventh principal component is simply "noise," paralleled in the real world by measurement error and other factors.

The correlations between the financial variables and the principal components also indicate that this data may be best described by a single factor. These correlation coefficients are sometimes called *component* or *factor loadings* because they describe which variables "load" or are correlated with which principal components. The correlations between the variables and the first principal component are all high, ranging from .671 to .963 (top right Table 3.2).

The correlations between the original variables and the new principal components may be found in one of two ways. First, because these values are truly correlation coefficients, the new or "predicted" scores for each case on each principal component can be found and correlated with the observations on the original variables. Another way is to simply multiply the eigenvectors by the square root of their associated eigenvalues:

$$L_{jk} = V_{jk}\sqrt{D_{kk}}$$

where $L_{jk}$ refers to variable $j$'s correlation with principal component $k$, $V_{jk}$ refers to variable $j$'s value on eigenvector $k$, and $D_{kk}$ indicates the $k$th eigenvalue. For example, number of chickens correlates with first principal component .876 ($.402\sqrt{4.741}$).

The new scores for each case in relation to the principal components are a linear combination of the data and the information contained in the basic structure. Because PCA performs an eigenanalysis on the cross-product matrix, these *component* or *factor scores* must be found by transforming the eigenvectors by their eigenvalues to create factor score coefficients and multiplying these values by the (standardized) original observations:

$$S_{ik} = \sum_{j} (V_{jk}/\sqrt{D_{kk}}) \cdot X_{ij}^*$$

where $S_{ik}$ is case $i$'s score on principal component $k$, $V_{jk}/\sqrt{D_{kk}}$ is the factor score coefficient for variable $j$ on principal component $k$, and $X_{ij}^*$ is case $i$'s standardized score on variable $j$. The factor scores, the values for each case on the new orthogonal axes, appear in Table 3.2. Thus case $a$'s score on the first principal component can be expressed as a linear combination of the original observations and the information contained in the basic structure:

$$S_{i1} = \sum_j (V_{j1}/\sqrt{D_{11}})X_{ij}^*$$

$$S_{11} = .402/2.17(-.789) + .394/2.17(-.834) + .334/2.17(-.089)$$
$$+ \ldots + .356/2.17(.120) = .822$$

Another way to get factor scores is simply to standardize the columns in the U matrix. Note that all of the above information can be conceptualized in terms of the basic structure in the data and can be obtained by factoring the data matrix directly. The basic structure of the column-standardized data is presented down the left-hand side of Table 3.2. In the top left are the component vectors for the financial variables; the middle panel contains the singular values; and the bottom left contains the component vectors for the households. This information can be transformed into the PCA results presented down the right-hand side of Table 3.2. Squaring the singular values and dividing by the number of households ($n - 1 = 19$) results in the eigenvalues. Multiplication of the component vectors (top left) by the square root of their eigenvalues results in the "factor loadings" (top right). Standardization of the component variables for the households (bottom left) results in the "factor scores" (bottom right).

Because the financial resource variables were simulated and the true household scores are known, we can test how well the first principal component represented the true scores. The correlation between the true scores (last column, Table 3.1) and the factor scores on the first principal component (first column, Table 3.2) is .823. Furthermore, the correlations between the variables and the first principal component (factor loadings) closely parallel the correlations of each variable with the true scores. Thus in this example the seven variables are quite well represented by the first principal component. Thus the linear combination of observed data on the original seven variables (i.e., the factor scores) can be used as an index of financial resources in other analyses.

## Multifactor Example

To illustrate multidimensional structure, we analyze data regarding the perceived effectiveness, safety, availability, and convenience of 15 contraceptive methods. In this example, respondents were asked to rank the methods from 1 to 15 for each concept. To simplify presentation and analysis, responses have been aggregated into groups representing the responses of seven individuals for each of the four ranking tasks with two groups per gender (see Table 3.3). Respondent groups are identified by task, effectiveness (E), safety (S), availability (A), convenience (C), and gender, female (F1, F2) and male (M1, M2), creating 16 respondent groups (EF1, EF2, EM1, EM2, SF1, SF2, etc.). To illustrate different analytical approaches and the effect of different data transformations prior to or during analysis, the contraceptive data will be analyzed first by the column variables, and second by the row variables. Finally, we will show that both of these analyses can give equivalent information if identical predecomposition transformations are used.

*Analysis of column variables.* A principal components analysis of the contraceptive methods based on their similarity in ratings of effectiveness, safety, availability, and convenience begins by correlating the columns in Table 3.3 with one another. The factor loadings, their eigenvalues, and the factor scores appear in Table 3.4 (only the first four factors are shown). The eigenvalues indicate that the similarity among methods accounts for 49.5% with one factor, 71.7% with two, and 80.5% with three. The loadings indicate that most of the methods correlate strongly with the first factor. The first factor scales hysterectomy, tubal ligation, and vasectomy at one end and douching, rhythm method, and withdrawal at the other.

To help understand the structure, the first two eigenvectors or factor loadings may be plotted (Figure 3.1). This structure is a function of the similarities and dissimilarities among the contraceptive methods with respect to availability, effectiveness, safety, and convenience. Similarities or strong correlations between methods across respondent groups cause the methods to "attract" one another and to be located near one another in the plotted configuration. Arrows are superimposed onto the diagram indicating items most correlated with each other. For example, a diaphragm is seen as most similar to an IUD. Item position in the spatial plot is also a function of "repelling" forces, so that even though abortion is most similar to tubal ligation, it is seen as very different from abstinence. Thus spatial propinquity represents an overall degree of similarity between methods.

Further insight is gained in the perceived similarity of contraceptive methods, by examination of the factor scores. In the spatial configuration (Figure 3.2), the principal axis (abscissa) appears to be a combina-

TABLE 3.3

Contraceptive Data

| | Pills | Condoms | IUD | Diaphrag | Foam | Rhythm | Abstin | Withdraw | Vasect | Tubal | Abortion | Douche | Oral Sex | Spermic | Hysterect |
|---|---|---|---|---|---|---|---|---|---|---|---|---|---|---|---|
| EF1 | 74 | 47 | 62 | 56 | 39 | 41 | 81 | 15 | 87 | 82 | 48 | 15 | 84 | 34 | 75 |
| EF2 | 77 | 57 | 60 | 63 | 44 | 23 | 92 | 24 | 83 | 83 | 28 | 21 | 66 | 39 | 80 |
| EM1 | 79 | 60 | 39 | 55 | 53 | 40 | 96 | 30 | 74 | 62 | 35 | 32 | 72 | 53 | 60 |
| EM2 | 51 | 62 | 81 | 68 | 62 | 39 | 44 | 57 | 69 | 76 | 45 | 36 | 41 | 56 | 53 |
| SF1 | 28 | 70 | 34 | 58 | 62 | 95 | 103 | 88 | 33 | 27 | 11 | 70 | 89 | 57 | 15 |
| SF2 | 28 | 80 | 26 | 61 | 54 | 85 | 92 | 83 | 61 | 41 | 16 | 60 | 82 | 43 | 28 |
| SM1 | 53 | 72 | 41 | 69 | 67 | 73 | 97 | 79 | 39 | 34 | 12 | 54 | 78 | 46 | 26 |
| SM2 | 74 | 85 | 78 | 70 | 57 | 62 | 71 | 62 | 39 | 38 | 30 | 40 | 41 | 51 | 42 |
| AF1 | 43 | 70 | 42 | 58 | 70 | 92 | 84 | 71 | 20 | 23 | 15 | 76 | 93 | 69 | 14 |
| AF2 | 54 | 71 | 37 | 48 | 69 | 75 | 92 | 93 | 26 | 21 | 26 | 69 | 86 | 59 | 14 |
| AM1 | 74 | 94 | 48 | 52 | 84 | 66 | 53 | 63 | 39 | 37 | 44 | 69 | 39 | 58 | 20 |
| AM2 | 54 | 89 | 56 | 89 | 60 | 68 | 45 | 67 | 40 | 45 | 42 | 49 | 54 | 47 | 35 |
| CF1 | 74 | 81 | 70 | 65 | 65 | 53 | 87 | 51 | 33 | 29 | 13 | 63 | 71 | 65 | 20 |
| CF2 | 66 | 66 | 60 | 50 | 52 | 42 | 80 | 69 | 56 | 49 | 14 | 53 | 76 | 55 | 52 |
| CM1 | 99 | 79 | 78 | 69 | 67 | 48 | 49 | 31 | 36 | 49 | 30 | 55 | 70 | 45 | 35 |
| CM2 | 45 | 56 | 79 | 76 | 63 | 62 | 61 | 49 | 51 | 65 | 36 | 56 | 47 | 55 | 39 |

TABLE 3.4

Results for Contraceptive Methods

| V Matrix, | Factor loadings | | | | | U Matrix, | Factor scores | | |
|---|---|---|---|---|---|---|---|---|---|
| | Fac1 | Fac2 | Fac3 | Fac4 | | Fac1 | Fac2 | Fac3 | Fac4 |
| Pills | −.534 | .305 | −.675 | .373 | EF1 | −1.897 | −1.119 | .100 | −.169 |
| Condoms | .575 | .553 | −.007 | .400 | EF2 | −1.688 | −.869 | −.160 | .586 |
| IUD | −.528 | .630 | −.128 | .015 | EM1 | −.876 | −.879 | −.945 | −.375 |
| Diaphrag | −.152 | .556 | .610 | .358 | EM2 | −.923 | 1.070 | .638 | −1.975 |
| Foam | .710 | .546 | −.222 | −.177 | SF1 | 1.313 | −1.112 | .698 | −.272 |
| Rhythm | .882 | −.089 | .346 | −.019 | SF2 | .643 | −1.127 | 1.613 | .442 |
| Abstin | .238 | −.889 | −.126 | .130 | SM1 | .649 | −.549 | .597 | 1.088 |
| Withdraw | .861 | −.060 | .292 | −.110 | SM2 | −.152 | .999 | .102 | 1.039 |
| Vasect | −.877 | −.324 | .138 | −.161 | AF1 | 1.415 | −.409 | −.431 | −.698 |
| Tubal | −.953 | −.031 | .140 | −.204 | AF2 | 1.179 | −.568 | −.710 | −.697 |
| Abortion | −.620 | .490 | .109 | −.322 | AM1 | .614 | 1.527 | −1.040 | −.944 |
| Douche | .947 | .145 | −.095 | −.088 | AM2 | .012 | 1.372 | 1.904 | 1.047 |
| Oral Sex | .320 | −.818 | −.120 | .168 | CF1 | .562 | .365 | −1.340 | .849 |
| Spermic | .667 | .218 | −.362 | −.418 | CF2 | −.148 | −.669 | −.911 | −.200 |
| Hysterec | −.963 | −.191 | .009 | −.011 | CM1 | −.349 | 1.142 | −1.102 | 1.604 |
| | | | | | CM2 | −.353 | .824 | .986 | −1.327 |
| Eigenvalues | 7.430 | 3.325 | 1.319 | .870 | | | | | |
| Proportion of Explained Variance | | | | | | | | | |
| | .495 | .222 | .088 | .058 | | | | | |

tion of available, safe, ineffective methods to less available, less safe, effective methods. The second dimension emphasizes gender differences in the interpretation of availability, convenience, and safety. For example, female respondents tended to rate abstinence as more convenient and more available than did males. Males considered the diaphragm to be more convenient than did females.

*Analysis of row variables.* PCA can also be performed on respondent groups. An analysis between observation units rather than variables is sometimes referred to as a "Q analysis." An assumption is that comparable units are being analyzed (McKeown and Thomas, 1988). In this case, because respondents rated each method on similar scales, the assumption is true.

The results of a PCA on respondent groups appear in Table 3.5. The first factor accounts for 44.1% of the variance, 66.1% is accounted for with two factors, and 81.6% with three. The factor loadings indicate a principal response pattern reflecting a combination of safety, availability, and convenience. By drawing trapezoidal shapes, connecting the

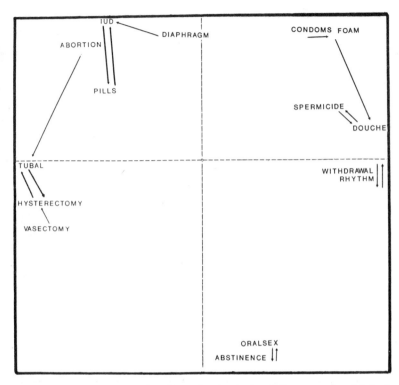

Figure 3.1. Plot of Factor Loadings for Analysis of Contraceptive Methods
(Table 3.4)

four respondent groups per task (Figure 3.3), we can see that respondents rated contraceptive methods similarly on these attributes. A second, smaller cluster is formed by the "effectiveness" responses. These two main respondent "clusters" are also evident by visual inspection of the correlation matrix.

The new scores for the contraceptive methods, the factor scores in relation to the first two dimensions in this reduced dimensionality, appear in Table 3.5 and in Figure 3.4. Contraceptive methods can be described in relation to one another and in relation to the principal components. For example, vasectomy is similar to tubal ligation in terms of the four attributes. Their low scores on the first principal component and high scores on the second principal component indicate that they are not thought to be safe, available, and convenient but are

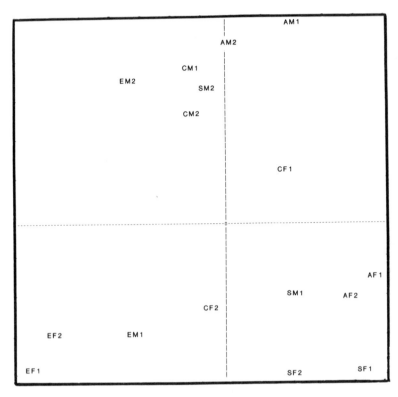

Figure 3.2. Plot of Factor Scores in Table 3.4

considered effective. Abstinence is both safe and effective. Rhythm and withdrawal methods, although safe and available, are not considered to be very effective.

*When row and column analyses provide identical information.* Above we saw that an analysis of Table 3.3 by column and row variables resulted in somewhat different results. This is because each analysis provided the basic structure of a different matrix: The analysis of column variables (R analysis) provided the basic structure of the data after the data had been standardized by columns, and the Q analysis analyzed Table 3.3 after row standardization. If a matrix were standardized by both row and column variables, both R and Q analyses would give equivalent results.

TABLE 3.5

Results of PCA for Respondent Groups

| U Matrix, Factor Loadings | | | | | V Matrix, Factor Scores | | | |
| | Fac1 | Fac2 | Fac3 | Fac4 | | Fac1 | Fac2 | Fac3 | Fac4 |
|---|---|---|---|---|---|---|---|---|---|
| EF1 | −.312 | .858 | −.265 | .028 | Pills | .064 | 1.156 | .461 | −2.678 |
| EF2 | −.179 | .957 | −.164 | .049 | Condoms | 1.203 | .261 | 1.055 | −.691 |
| EM1 | .124 | .843 | −.403 | −.165 | IUD | −.219 | .724 | 1.918 | .606 |
| EM2 | −.248 | .446 | .656 | .430 | Diaphrag | .423 | .408 | 1.301 | 1.131 |
| SF1 | .894 | −.164 | −.338 | .230 | Foam | .491 | −.336 | .679 | −.294 |
| SF2 | .794 | −.033 | −.395 | .344 | Rhythm | .800 | −1.234 | −.219 | .562 |
| SM1 | .945 | .116 | −.211 | .139 | Abstin | 1.211 | 1.320 | −1.644 | .392 |
| SM2 | .667 | .322 | .508 | −.091 | Withdraw | .794 | −1.326 | −.295 | .956 |
| AF1 | .917 | −.210 | −.202 | .021 | Vasect | −1.068 | .866 | −.645 | .835 |
| AF2 | .916 | −.202 | −.281 | −.055 | Tubal | −1.192 | .814 | .266 | 1.174 |
| AM1 | .677 | −.248 | .398 | −.387 | Abortion | −1.845 | −1.509 | −.127 | −.839 |
| AM2 | .648 | −.090 | .538 | .114 | Douche | .318 | −1.518 | −.252 | −.578 |
| CF1 | .878 | .291 | .144 | −.201 | Oral Sex | .723 | .559 | −1.675 | −.263 |
| CF2 | .644 | .547 | −.246 | .006 | Spermic | −.045 | −.566 | −.027 | −.174 |
| CM1 | .438 | .460 | .490 | −.488 | Hysterec | −1.659 | .380 | −.797 | −.138 |
| CM2 | .379 | .237 | .580 | .530 | | | | | |

Eigenvalues

| | 7.052 | 3.512 | 2.488 | 1.141 |
|---|---|---|---|---|

Proportion of Explained Variance

| | .441 | .220 | .155 | .071 |
|---|---|---|---|---|

Table 3.6 contains the data from Table 3.3, except they have been standardized by rows *and* columns (with 30 iterations). (Standardization was performed with the descriptive standard deviation.) Across the top panel of Table 3.7 appear the first four components (U and V) resulting from a singular value decomposition of the double-standardized contraceptive data. The singular values appear under the corresponding characteristic vectors. A PCA of the data in Table 3.6 with respondent group as the unit of analysis (by rows) would result in the information displayed down the left-hand side of Table 3.7. Thus the top left set of eigenvectors can be obtained from a singular value decomposition of the data or from a PCA of the correlations between respondent groups. The eigenvalues resulting from a PCA of row variables are equal to the square of the singular value divided by the number of columns (e.g., $9.950^2/15 = 6.599$). The results of a PCA of the contraceptive methods appear down the right-hand side of Table 3.7. The eigenvectors appearing in the top right-hand side of the table can

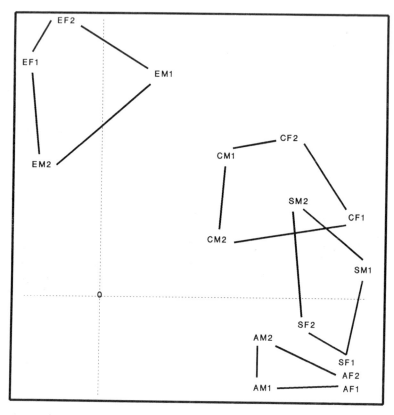

Figure 3.3. Plot of Factor Loadings for Analysis of Respondent Groups

be obtained directly with an SVD or by performing a PCA on the correlations among contraceptive methods. Factor loadings (middle panel, Table 3.7) are obtained by multiplying the eigenvectors by the square root of their eigenvalues.

Factor scores obtained from a PCA of row variables are equivalent to the eigenvectors obtained from a column analysis, except that they have been standardized to a mean of zero and a standard deviation of one. Thus if the contraceptive eigenvectors in the upper right-hand side of Table 3.7 are standardized by columns (multiplied by $n - 1$), one would obtain the factor scores in the lower left corner. Or, if the factor scores in the lower left corner were normed to unit length (divided by $n - 1$) they would be equal to the eigenvectors in the upper right-hand corner. Similarly, the factor scores for row variables obtained from an

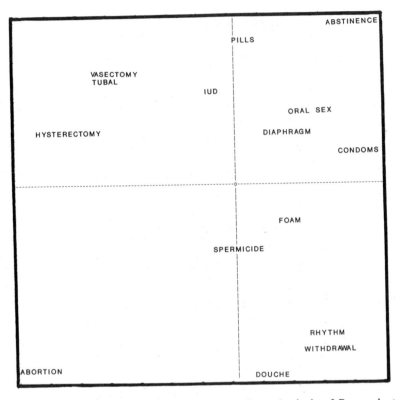

Figure 3.4. Plot of Factor Scores of Methods From Analysis of Respondent
Groups (Table 3.5)

analysis of column variables are equivalent to the eigenvectors resulting from an analysis of row variables.

Only one pair of plots (contraceptive methods and respondent
groups) are presented, because they are equivalent up to a scale factor
and reflection for both R and Q analyses. Figure 3.5 is a spatial plot of
the similarity of contraceptive methods obtained by plotting the factor
loadings for the contraceptive methods. Figure 3.6 is a plot of the factor
scores for the respondent groups.

The double standardization of the contraceptive data allows the
relationship between the basic structure of a matrix and the cross
product of that matrix to hold true for correlation matrices. If Z repre-

TABLE 3.6

Double-Standardized Contraceptive Data

| | Pills | Condoms | IUD | Diaphrag | Foam | Rhythm | Abstin | Withdraw | Vaseet | Tubal | Abortion | Douche | Oral Sex | Spermic | Hysterec |
|---|---|---|---|---|---|---|---|---|---|---|---|---|---|---|---|
| EF1 | .507 | -1.076 | .250 | -.263 | -1.328 | -.464 | .268 | -1.095 | 1.418 | 1.280 | 1.079 | -1.390 | .628 | -1.145 | 1.331 |
| EF2 | .649 | -.727 | .203 | .057 | -1.182 | -1.192 | .601 | -1.012 | 1.448 | 1.464 | .239 | -1.353 | .108 | -.965 | 1.660 |
| EM1 | .859 | -.964 | -.824 | -.682 | -.899 | -1.047 | .867 | -1.349 | 1.398 | .843 | .620 | -1.390 | .250 | 1.128 | 1.190 |
| EM2 | -.472 | -.859 | 1.138 | .330 | .072 | -1.151 | -1.428 | -.188 | 1.157 | 1.560 | 1.336 | -1.181 | -1.251 | .088 | .847 |
| SF1 | -1.486 | -.197 | -1.060 | -.455 | .094 | 1.696 | 1.146 | .186 | -.651 | -.866 | -1.027 | 1.155 | 1.030 | .437 | -.999 |
| SF2 | -1.655 | .749 | -1.578 | -.183 | -.807 | 1.465 | .843 | 1.211 | .909 | -.162 | -.748 | .667 | .868 | -1.203 | -.373 |
| SM1 | -.537 | .024 | -1.128 | .722 | 1.111 | 1.026 | 1.453 | 1.383 | -.632 | -.902 | -1.601 | .238 | .836 | -1.198 | -.794 |
| SM2 | 1.002 | 1.638 | 1.635 | .840 | -.731 | .101 | -.372 | .142 | -.695 | -.645 | .377 | -1.362 | -2.005 | -.358 | .427 |
| AF1 | -.861 | -.290 | -.750 | -.522 | .815 | 1.385 | .241 | .324 | -1.351 | -1.121 | -.815 | 1.378 | 1.083 | 1.595 | -1.109 |
| AF2 | -.370 | -.158 | -1.051 | -1.398 | .923 | .748 | .720 | 1.540 | -1.172 | -1.347 | -.047 | 1.182 | .952 | .702 | -1.220 |
| AM1 | .421 | 1.406 | -.568 | -1.058 | 2.202 | .050 | -1.113 | -.105 | -.536 | -.557 | 1.030 | .832 | -1.404 | .329 | -.929 |
| AM2 | -.476 | 1.478 | -.138 | 2.369 | -.285 | .330 | -1.735 | .238 | -.524 | -.124 | 1.254 | -.431 | -.830 | -.953 | -.177 |
| CF1 | .799 | .894 | .819 | .076 | .516 | -.683 | .581 | -.700 | -1.159 | -1.323 | -1.483 | .925 | .170 | 1.863 | -1.296 |
| CF2 | .556 | -.642 | .412 | -1.684 | -1.501 | -1.443 | .403 | .857 | .892 | .405 | -1.386 | .292 | .824 | .579 | 1.439 |
| CM1 | 2.165 | .602 | 1.197 | .494 | .760 | -.845 | -1.481 | -1.658 | -.720 | .180 | .280 | .157 | .145 | -1.162 | -.116 |
| CM2 | -1.100 | -1.876 | 1.443 | 1.357 | .239 | .024 | -.994 | -.774 | .219 | 1.313 | .890 | .280 | -1.403 | .264 | .117 |

TABLE 3.7

Results From Double-Standardized Data

| U Matrix, Eigenvectors | | | | | V Matrix, Eigenvectors | | | |
|---|---|---|---|---|---|---|---|---|
| | Fac1 | Fac2 | Fac3 | Fac4 | | Fac1 | Fac2 | Fac3 | Fac4 |
| EF1 | −.315 | −.257 | .092 | .063 | Pills | −.197 | .126 | −.480 | .427 |
| EF2 | −.330 | −.256 | .022 | .157 | Condoms | .132 | .343 | .027 | .548 |
| EM1 | −.237 | −.300 | −.227 | −.070 | IUD | −.262 | .255 | −.199 | −.025 |
| EM2 | −.325 | .080 | .101 | −.362 | Diaphrag | −.113 | .311 | .403 | .093 |
| SF1 | .354 | −.170 | .140 | −.101 | Foam | .222 | .330 | −.114 | −.259 |
| SF2 | .205 | −.251 | .437 | .166 | Rhythm | .320 | .027 | .377 | −.052 |
| SM1 | .290 | −.087 | .236 | .248 | Abstin | .186 | −.426 | −.066 | .199 |
| SM2 | −.142 | .326 | .030 | .407 | Withdraw | .296 | −.109 | .270 | .057 |
| AF1 | .348 | −.010 | −.130 | −.260 | Vasect | −.289 | −.336 | .141 | −.061 |
| AF2 | .350 | −.057 | −.106 | −.122 | Tubal | −.358 | −.148 | .133 | −.239 |
| AM1 | .110 | .365 | −.143 | −.148 | Abortion | −.269 | .221 | .186 | −.273 |
| AM2 | −.068 | .368 | .428 | .147 | Douche | .350 | .055 | −.119 | −.217 |
| CF1 | .181 | .161 | −.500 | .109 | Oral Sex | .201 | −.397 | −.086 | .134 |
| CF2 | −.077 | −.381 | −.306 | .108 | Spermic | .133 | −.016 | −.490 | −.430 |
| CM1 | −.155 | .318 | −.241 | .255 | Hysterec | −.351 | −.238 | .015 | .098 |
| CM2 | −.189 | .150 | .167 | −.596 | | | | | |

Singular Values

| | | | | | | | | |
|---|---|---|---|---|---|---|---|---|
| | 9.950 | 7.086 | 5.415 | 4.416 | | 9.950 | 7.086 | 5.415 | 4.416 |

Singular Values

Eigenvalues (Rows)

| | | | | | | | | |
|---|---|---|---|---|---|---|---|---|
| | 6.559 | 3.348 | 1.956 | 1.300 | | 6.188 | 3.138 | 1.833 | 1.219 |

Eigenvalues (Cols)

Proportion of Explained Variance

| | | | | | | | | |
|---|---|---|---|---|---|---|---|---|
| | .412 | .209 | .122 | .081 | | .413 | .209 | .122 | .081 |

Proportion of Explained Variance

(continued)

sents a matrix with row and column means equal to zero and within-row and within-column variances equal to one, then

$$Z = UdV^T$$

$$R = \frac{1}{n}Z^TZ = V \cdot \frac{1}{n}d^2V^T$$

$$Q = \frac{1}{m}ZZ^T = U \cdot \frac{1}{m}d^2U^T$$

where $d^{1/2}/n$ indicates the square root of the eigenvalue divided by the number of observations. Because the descriptive formula for variance was used to standardize the data, $1/n$ and $1/m$ are the appropriate correction factors.

TABLE 3.7

Continued

| U Matrix, Factor Loadings | | | | | V Matrix, Factor Loadings | | | |
|---|---|---|---|---|---|---|---|---|
| | Fac1 | Fac2 | Fac3 | Fac4 | | Fac1 | Fac2 | Fac3 | Fac4 |
| EF1 | −.808 | .470 | −.129 | .071 | Pills | −.491 | .224 | −.650 | .471 |
| EF2 | −.847 | .468 | −.030 | .179 | Condoms | .329 | .607 | .037 | .605 |
| EM1 | −.607 | .549 | .317 | −.080 | IUD | −.651 | .453 | −.270 | −.027 |
| EM2 | −.835 | −.145 | −.141 | −.413 | Diaphrag | −.282 | .551 | .546 | .103 |
| SF1 | .909 | .310 | −.195 | −.115 | Foam | .551 | .585 | −.155 | −.286 |
| SF2 | .528 | .459 | −.612 | .190 | Rhythm | .797 | .048 | .511 | −.057 |
| SM1 | .745 | .159 | −.331 | .283 | Abstin | .463 | −.755 | −.089 | .220 |
| SM2 | −.364 | −.596 | −.042 | .465 | Withdraw | .736 | −.193 | .365 | .063 |
| AF1 | .895 | .017 | .181 | −.297 | Vasect | −.718 | −.595 | .192 | −.068 |
| AF2 | .899 | .104 | .149 | −.140 | Tubal | −.891 | −.262 | .180 | −.264 |
| AM1 | .282 | −.668 | .201 | −.169 | Abortion | −.670 | .392 | .252 | −.302 |
| AM2 | −.175 | −.675 | −.599 | .167 | Douche | .872 | .098 | −.161 | −.240 |
| CF1 | .465 | −.295 | .699 | .124 | Oral Sex | .501 | −.704 | −.116 | .148 |
| CF2 | −.198 | .696 | .428 | .124 | Spermic | .330 | −.028 | −.663 | −.475 |
| CM1 | −.400 | −.582 | .337 | .291 | Hysterec | −.874 | −.421 | .020 | .109 |
| CM2 | −.486 | −.275 | −.234 | −.680 | | | | | |

| V Matrix, Factor Scores | | | | | U Matrix, Factor Scores | | | |
|---|---|---|---|---|---|---|---|---|
| | Fac1 | Fac2 | Fac3 | Fac4 | | Fac1 | Fac2 | Fac3 | Fac4 |
| Pills | −.739 | −.473 | 1.796 | 1.598 | EF1 | −1.220 | −.995 | .357 | .243 |
| Condoms | .493 | −1.283 | −.103 | 2.049 | EF2 | −1.279 | −.991 | .084 | .607 |
| IUD | −.979 | −.955 | .745 | −.092 | EM1 | −.916 | −1.162 | −.879 | −.272 |
| Diaphrag | −.425 | −1.163 | −1.510 | .349 | EM2 | −1.259 | .309 | .391 | −1.402 |
| Foam | .828 | −1.236 | .428 | −.970 | SF1 | 1.370 | −.657 | .541 | −.392 |
| Rhythm | 1.198 | −.103 | −1.412 | −.195 | SF2 | .795 | −.972 | 1.694 | .644 |
| Abstin | .697 | 1.593 | .246 | .747 | SM1 | 1.123 | −.337 | .916 | .961 |
| Withdraw | 1.106 | .407 | −1.009 | .213 | SM2 | −.549 | 1.262 | .117 | 1.578 |
| Vasect | −1.079 | 1.258 | −.529 | −.229 | AF1 | 1.349 | −.038 | −.502 | −1.008 |
| Tubal | −1.340 | .555 | −.497 | −.896 | AF2 | 1.354 | −.221 | −.411 | −.474 |
| Abortion | −1.008 | −.827 | −.696 | −1.023 | AM1 | .425 | 1.413 | −.555 | −.573 |
| Douche | 1.311 | −.208 | .445 | −.814 | AM2 | −.264 | 1.427 | 1.657 | .569 |
| Oral Sex | .755 | 1.486 | .321 | .501 | CF1 | .702 | .623 | −1.936 | .422 |
| Spermic | .496 | .058 | 1.833 | −1.608 | CF2 | −.299 | −1.474 | −1.187 | .419 |
| Hysterec | −1.315 | .890 | −.057 | .368 | CM1 | −.602 | 1.231 | −.934 | .988 |
| | | | | | CM2 | −.731 | .583 | .648 | −2.309 |

This same relationship holds true for the analysis of other cross-product matrices. If the data matrix is double-centered (C), so that row and column means are zero, a PCA of either the row or column cross-product matrices ($CC^T$, $C^TC$) provides complimentary information: $C = UdV^T$, $R = C^TC = Vd^2V^T$, $Q = CC^T = Ud^2U^T$. Burt (1937) referred

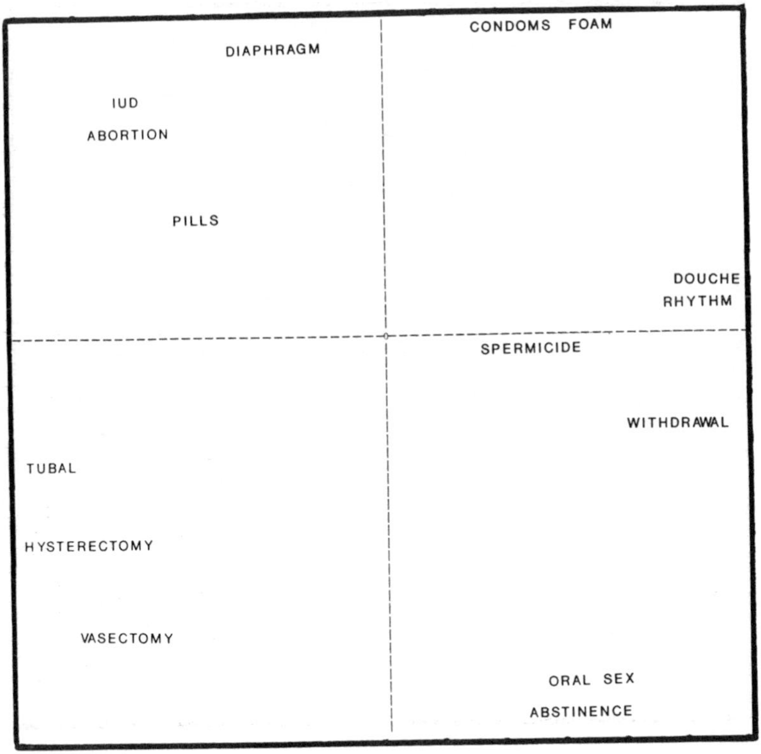

Figure 3.5. Plot of Factor Loadings From Column Analysis

to this as an analysis of "unaveraged" covariances. PCA on an "averaged" covariance matrix produces similar results:

$$Q = \frac{1}{m}CC^T = U \cdot \frac{1}{m}d^2 U^T$$

$$R = \frac{1}{n}C^T C = V \cdot \frac{1}{n}d^2 V^T$$

Typically, PCA is described in terms of factoring a cross-product matrix (e.g., a correlation matrix) to obtain column variable eigenvectors and eigenvalues. Then the eigenvectors, eigenvalues, and (standardized) data are used to solve for the row variable eigenvectors (factor scores). Here, we saw that PCA can be described in terms of the basic structure in a data matrix: Row and column variable "component vectors" can be obtained directly by decomposition of the data, and factor scores and factor loadings are simply transformed versions of

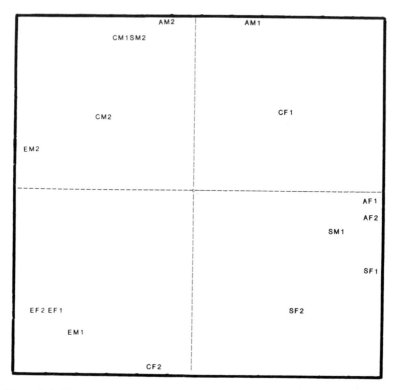

Figure 3.6. Plot of Factor Scores for Respondent Groups From Column Analysis

those component vectors. Viewing PCA in this way it is also evident that the distinction between R-type and Q-type PCA is somewhat artificial and due to transformations performed prior to decomposition of the data. Thus PCA provides the basic structure of column variables in relation to the underlying component variables and of row variables in relation to the underlying component variables.

## 4. MULTIDIMENSIONAL PREFERENCE SCALING

Multidimensional preference scaling (MDPREF) provides information equivalent to a PCA in that a data matrix is factored to its basic structure in order to describe the data more parsimoniously with the underlying, component variables. However, PCA provides information only on the basic structure of the row variables or the column variables in relation to the latent vectors, but no attempt is made to bring the row and column configurations into similar "units" or into the same spatial configuration. In fact, interpreting PCA output with reference to plots of factor loadings and factor scores probably *feels* like these configurations are intimately related and that interpretation might be much easier if somehow the configurations were in "similar units" so they could be "superimposed." MDPREF and correspondence analysis (CA) are designed to present row and column variables in the *same* configuration. MDPREF and CA are "dual-scaling" or "joint-space" procedures that allow one to examine: (1) the structure among column variables, (2) the structure among row variables, and (3) the structure of the row *and* column variables together, that is, the space occupied jointly by both. The dual-scaling of row and column variables is achieved somewhat differently in the two methods. We begin with a description of MDPREF, because it serves as a natural link between the more widely used and understood method of PCA and the newest addition to the family of metric scaling techniques, CA.

MDPREF is a sister of PCA and perhaps best described or thought of as a variation of PCA. It belongs to the family of "unfolding" scaling models (Carroll, 1972). As we shall illustrate in this chapter, MDPREF provides information identical to that of a PCA, *if* identical preanalysis data transformations are used. The main departure from PCA is that row variables are transformed and "fit" as vectors into the column variable configuration. To illustrate the identities between PCA and MDPREF, we reanalyze the contraceptive data in the previous chapter, first, standardized by rows; second, standardized by columns; and third, double-centered.

*With row standardization.* MDPREF (Chang and Carroll, 1968) offers two options for preanalysis normalization of data, namely, a correction for row means or standardization within *rows*. Here we describe an analysis of the contraceptive data standardized within rows (with the inferential standard deviation). This data set, after standardization, is the data that will be analyzed and is called the "first score matrix." The basic structure matrices resulting from factorization of the first score matrix appear in Table 4.1 (only the first four factors are presented). This analysis parallels the PCA Q-analysis of row-standardized data in the last chapter. The U matrix latent variables in Table 4.1 are identical to the U matrix eigenvectors in the previous analysis (except for a reflection of the first, third, and fourth factors). The column latent variables (**V** matrix) in Table 4.1, if standardized, would be identical to the factor scores in Table 3.5. The singular values in Table 4.1 when squared and divided by the number of column variables ($m - 1 = 14$) are equal to the eigenvalues in Table 3.5. Because MDPREF (Chang and Carroll, 1968) finds the basic structure matrices with an eigenanalysis of cross-product matrices, the "latent roots" that are reported are the squared singular values. Explained variance as estimated from the eigenvalues of a cross-product matrix of standardized data is equivalent to that estimated from the eigenvalues of a correlation matrix. Thus the first two factors explain 66.1% of the variance as they did with PCA.

The **V** matrix of latent vectors for the column variables form the central, stimulus configuration. (These are analogous to the factor scores from the PCA Q-analysis.) The row variables are fit into the $k$-dimensional column variable structure by estimating the subjects' (row) response vectors in $k$ dimensions. To do this, the basic structure matrices are used to reconstruct the data, as in Example 2.3:

$$\hat{\mathbf{X}}_k = \mathbf{U}_k^T \mathbf{D}_k \mathbf{V}_k$$

where $\mathbf{U}_k$, $\mathbf{D}_k$, and $\mathbf{V}_k$ represent the first $k$ factors, and $\mathbf{X}_k$ is the $k$-dimensional estimate of the data. The estimated responses ($\hat{\mathbf{X}}_k$) are then normed to unit length within rows ($\hat{\mathbf{X}}^*$):

$$\hat{X}_{ij}^* = \hat{X}_{ij} \left/ \left( \sum_j \hat{X}_{ij}^2 \right)^{1/2} \right. \quad \text{where } j = 1, m \text{ columns}$$

A two-dimensional estimate can be obtained from the information in Table 4.1. The first two row latent vectors (the first two columns in the **U** matrix in Table 4.1), the first two singular values (these are actually not necessary, because of the unit norming that follows), and the first two column latent vectors (the first two columns in the **V** matrix) are multiplied together to obtain $\hat{\mathbf{X}}$. The rows in $\hat{\mathbf{X}}$ are the "predicted" responses for the respondent groups, in terms of the first two latent vectors. The predicted responses are then normalized to unit length for each respondent group, so that the predicted response vector is in the same scale as the stimulus configuration. The predicted responses in $k$ dimensions are called the "second score matrix" (see Table 4.2).

In order to locate the predicted response vectors in the stimulus configuration, the coordinates of the vector termini are found by mul-

TABLE 4.1

Basic Structure Information for Row-Standardized Data

| U Matrix | | | | | V Matrix | | | |
|---|---|---|---|---|---|---|---|---|
| | Fac1 | Fac2 | Fac3 | Fac4 | | Fac1 | Fac2 | Fac3 | Fac4 |
| EF1 | .118 | .458 | .168 | −.026 | Pills | −.017 | .309 | −.123 | .716 |
| EF2 | .068 | .511 | .104 | −.046 | Condoms | −.321 | .070 | −.282 | .185 |
| EM1 | −.047 | .450 | .255 | .154 | IUD | .058 | .193 | −.513 | −.162 |
| EM2 | .093 | .238 | −.416 | −.402 | Diaphrag | −.113 | .109 | −.348 | −.302 |
| SF1 | −.337 | −.087 | .215 | −.215 | Foam | −.131 | −.090 | −.181 | .079 |
| SF2 | −.299 | −.018 | .251 | −.322 | Rhythm | −.214 | −.330 | .058 | −.150 |
| SM1 | −.356 | .062 | .134 | −.130 | Abstin | −.324 | .353 | .439 | −.105 |
| SM2 | −.251 | .172 | −.322 | .085 | Withdraw | −.212 | −.354 | .079 | −.255 |
| AF1 | −.345 | −.112 | .128 | −.020 | Vasect | .285 | .231 | .172 | −.223 |
| AF2 | −.345 | −.108 | .178 | .052 | Tubal | .319 | .218 | −.071 | −.314 |
| AM1 | −.255 | −.132 | −.252 | .362 | Abortion | .493 | −.403 | .034 | .224 |
| AM2 | −.244 | −.048 | −.341 | −.107 | Douche | −.085 | −.406 | .067 | .155 |
| CF1 | −.331 | .155 | −.091 | .188 | Oral Sex | −.193 | .149 | .448 | .070 |
| CF2 | −.242 | .292 | .156 | −.006 | Spermic | .012 | −.151 | .007 | .047 |
| CM1 | −.165 | .246 | −.311 | .457 | Hysterec | .443 | .101 | .213 | .037 |
| CM2 | −.143 | .126 | −.368 | −.497 | | | | | |

Singular Values:

| | | | |
|---|---|---|---|
| 9.936 | 7.012 | 5.901 | 3.996 |

MDPREF Latent Roots:

| | | | |
|---|---|---|---|
| 98.733 | 49.172 | 34.826 | 15.970 |

Proportion of Explained Variance:

| | | | |
|---|---|---|---|
| .441 | .220 | .155 | .071 |

tiplying the predicted responses by the stimulus coordinates, or by stretching the U configuration (**Ud**) norming within *rows* (**Ud***):

$$\hat{X}_k^* V_k = (Ud)_k^*$$

The two-dimensional coordinates for the predicted responses appear in Table 4.3. The dual-scaling plot of row and column variables appears as Figure 4.1.

The interpretation of the dimensions and of the stimulus configuration is facilitated with the dual-scaling of both stimuli and respondent groups in the same configuration. In MDPREF, the column stimuli form the "center" of the configuration and the row respondent groups (the terminal tips of the vectors) are displayed on the "outside" of the configuration. Subject response vectors are identified by their terminal

TABLE 4.2
Predicted Responses

Second Score Matrix

| | Pills | Condom | IUD | Diaphrag | Foam | Rhythm | Abstin | Withdraw | Vasect | Tubal | Abortion | Douche | Oral Sex | Spermic | Hysterec |
|---|---|---|---|---|---|---|---|---|---|---|---|---|---|---|---|
| EF1 | .285 | -.044 | .202 | .064 | -.129 | -.383 | .221 | -.406 | .315 | .313 | -.210 | -.410 | .074 | -.138 | .247 |
| EF2 | .301 | .009 | .201 | .086 | -.113 | -.363 | .287 | -.387 | .280 | .273 | -.305 | -.414 | .111 | -.146 | .181 |
| EM1 | .308 | .116 | .183 | .124 | -.070 | -.295 | .396 | -.320 | .187 | .169 | -.471 | -.389 | .176 | -.151 | .036 |
| EM2 | .262 | -.095 | .197 | .040 | -.142 | -.392 | .151 | -.413 | .341 | .345 | -.113 | -.396 | .037 | -.126 | .304 |
| SF1 | -.039 | .304 | -.092 | .092 | .145 | .270 | .255 | .273 | -.323 | -.353 | -.412 | .157 | .163 | .016 | -.454 |
| SF2 | .004 | .318 | -.066 | .108 | .135 | .227 | .309 | .227 | -.295 | -.327 | -.476 | .102 | .187 | -.006 | -.447 |
| SM1 | .055 | .328 | -.035 | .126 | .119 | .172 | .364 | .168 | -.255 | -.290 | -.538 | .035 | .210 | -.030 | -.428 |
| SM2 | .150 | .320 | .031 | .149 | .079 | .049 | .445 | .037 | -.157 | -.193 | -.619 | -.100 | .239 | -.076 | -.355 |
| AF1 | -.052 | .298 | -.100 | .086 | .148 | .282 | .237 | .286 | -.330 | -.359 | -.390 | .173 | .155 | .022 | -.455 |
| AF2 | -.050 | .299 | -.099 | .087 | .148 | .280 | .240 | .284 | -.329 | -.358 | -.395 | .170 | .156 | .021 | -.455 |
| AM1 | -.090 | .278 | -.121 | .069 | .154 | .314 | .182 | .321 | -.348 | -.374 | -.324 | .219 | .130 | .041 | -.451 |
| AM2 | -.026 | .309 | -.084 | .097 | .142 | .257 | .272 | .259 | -.315 | -.346 | -.433 | .140 | .171 | .009 | -.453 |
| CF1 | .113 | .327 | .005 | .142 | .096 | .099 | .418 | .090 | -.198 | -.234 | -.595 | -.047 | .230 | -.059 | -.389 |
| CF2 | .213 | .290 | .081 | .157 | .042 | -.050 | .475 | -.068 | -.068 | -.102 | -.637 | -.198 | .244 | -.107 | -.272 |
| CM1 | .236 | .272 | .100 | .157 | .025 | -.091 | .479 | -.110 | -.029 | -.062 | -.632 | -.235 | .241 | -.118 | -.232 |
| CM2 | .178 | .310 | .053 | .154 | .064 | .007 | .461 | -.008 | -.119 | -.155 | -.632 | -.143 | .243 | -.090 | -.322 |

TABLE 4.3

Coordinates of Response Vector Terminal Points

U Matrix, After Vector-Fitting

|  | Fac1 | Fac2 |
|---|---|---|
| EF1 | .342 | .940 |
| EF2 | .184 | .983 |
| EM1 | −.145 | .989 |
| EM2 | .486 | .874 |
| SF1 | −.984 | −.180 |
| SF2 | −.999 | −.042 |
| SM1 | −.993 | .122 |
| SM2 | −.901 | .434 |
| AF1 | −.975 | −.223 |
| AF2 | −.976 | −.216 |
| AM1 | −.939 | −.344 |
| AM2 | −.991 | −.137 |
| CF1 | −.949 | .314 |
| CF2 | −.762 | .647 |
| CM1 | −.690 | .724 |
| CM2 | −.848 | .530 |

tips, displayed here in a two-dimensional model, along an arc on the outer edge of the configuration. An estimate of each response vector can be drawn into the figure by drawing a line from the terminus end through the origin. Each vector extends the diameter of a unit radius circle, passing through the origin. Interpretation of an individual vector is obtained by moving down the length of the vector, drawing perpendicular lines between the stimuli and the vector. For example, the rankings of the contraceptive methods for safety (see SF2) ordered condom as safest (if a perpendicular line is dropped from abstinence to the SF2 response vector, it is closest to the tip of the SF2 vector), followed by abstinence, withdrawal, rhythm, . . . tubal ligation, hysterectomy, and abortion. (This ordering corresponds to the values in row SF2 of Table 4.2.)

The correlation between respondent groups is indicated by the size of the angle between their vectors: angles less than 90 degrees indicate positive correlations, 90 degree angles indicate zero correlation, and angles between 90 and 180 degrees indicate a negative correlation. Similarly, the correlation between response vectors and the factors is indicated by the angle between them. Thus the first factor or dimension is most like the concept of safety, but is also a combination of safety,

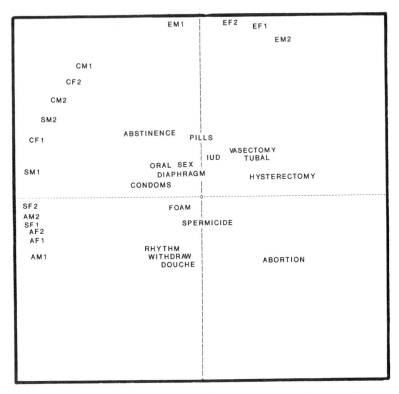

Figure 4.1. MDPREF Representation of Contraceptive Methods and Respondent Groups for Row-Standardized Data

availability, and convenience. The location of the four respondent groups (EM1, EF2, etc.) near the second dimension, the ordinate, indicates that it is best interpreted as "effectiveness." The configuration of contraceptive methods in Figure 4.1 is equivalent to that in Figure 3.4 except for a scale factor and a reflection of the first dimension. Also, the configuration of respondent groups in Figure 4.1 is analogous to that in Figure 3.3.

The first dimension of MDPREF is sometimes called the "popularity" or "consensus" dimension, because it represents the overall aggregation of subject responses. In the case of high agreement among respondents, MDPREF simply displays that concordance spatially, by fanning out the subject response vectors around the first dimension. In the contraceptive example, the intercorrelation among the concepts of availability, safety, and convenience dominates the structure, and those response vectors lie within 60 degrees of one another and the first dimension.

In PCA this first factor is sometimes called a "magnitude" factor, because it contains information on the magnitude of row and column variables (i.e., their totals or means). In some cases, an analysis is performed simply to retrieve the magnitude factor. For example, column variables may all represent or measure different aspects of the same underlying construct. We illustrated this with the "financial resources" scale in the PCA chapter. In the case of high concordance among informants, a kind of PCA can be used to estimate subjects' "competencies" and then an optimal aggregation of responses (the consensus dimension) can be found (Batchelder and Romney, 1988; Romney, Batchelder, and Weller, 1987; Romney, Weller, and Batchelder, 1986).

To illustrate the difference between a "magnitude" factor and other factors, we use a partitioning of variance analogy. The total variance in a matrix (i.e., in the ANOVA sense of the total sum of squares divided by the number of observations) can be partitioned into main effects (row and column variable effects) and into interaction/error variance. Such a partitioning of variance is appropriate for a data set that can be considered either as a two-way ANOVA with one observation per cell or a one-way ANOVA with repeated measures. Thus with ANOVA terminology, the multidimensional structure present in data can be described in terms of a "main effects" factor, "interactive" factors, and error. The main effects in a data matrix are due to differences among row or column means (totals). Depending upon transformations performed upon the data prior to analysis, the first component will contain information regarding main effects. For example, if the first singular value is relatively large it can indicate that much of the original data may be accounted for or reconstructed from the information in the row and column means (or totals).

Different transformations of the data allow the researcher to examine different aspects of the underlying, basic structure. Structure may be examined "wholistically" with main effects, interaction, and error present or the main effects can be "removed" to examine interaction (and error). A row or column effect can be removed with a transformation that sets row or column means (totals) to equal values. Centering or standardization of row *or* column variables results in a partial removal of the main effects, by setting one set of means to zero. Double-centering and double standardization removes both sets of means. Removal of the "magnitude" or "popularity" dimension allows the researcher to examine the data for patterns of "interactive" structure. In PCA and MDPREF this may be accomplished with data transformations prior to analysis. In correspondence analysis, it is done implicitly with the "square-root" transformation.

Centering or standardization within respondent groups (rows) removes differences in row means, but allows differences in column means to remain. Thus the "consensus" pattern among respondents, characterized by differences in the column means, remains relatively unaffected. Because of this, the first dimension or factor in MDPREF and PCA Q-analysis after row centering or row standardization reflects the major, consensual response pattern.

*With column standardization.* Column standardization also removes only one set of means; column means are set to zero. Although within-column transformations of data are not usually performed prior to an MDPREF, we present an analysis of column-standardized data to illustrate the similarity of MDPREF to a PCA of column variables. The basic structure matrices for the column-standardized contraceptive data appear here in Table 4.4. The results parallel the PCA on column-standardized data. The two-dimensional coordinates for the respondent group vector tips, the stretched and row-normed U matrix also appear in Table 4.4 (U matrix, after vector-fittings). The MDPREF configuration (Figure 4.2) for contraceptive methods is identical to that provided by a PCA and the respondent group configuration parallels the PCA results presented in Figure 3.2.

*With double-centering.* Centering of data, usually performed on column *or* row variables, is analogous to analyzing a covariance matrix. Data are sometimes double-centered to remove the magnitude or popularity dimension (Green, 1973). The results of an MDPREF analysis on the double-centered contraceptive data appear in Figure 4.3. Results from column-standardized and double-centered analyses are quite similar. This in large part is due to the removal of the differences among column means. Because the data were originally collected by ranking the contraceptive methods from 1 to 15, there were no differences in row totals (means). Thus column standardization would remove differences in column means and leave minimal differences in row means.

PCA and MDPREF on row- *or* column-standardized data will usually contain information regarding differences in magnitude among variables in the first factor. The predominant response pattern in the con-

TABLE 4.4

Basic Structure of Column-Standardized Data

| U Matrix | | | U Matrix After Vector-Fittings | | | V Matrix | | |
|---|---|---|---|---|---|---|---|---|
| | Fac1 | Fac2 | | Fac1 | Fac2 | | Fac1 | Fac2 |
| EF1 | −.490 | −.289 | EF1 | −.930 | −.367 | Pills | −.196 | .167 |
| EF2 | −.436 | −.224 | EF2 | −.946 | −.326 | Condoms | .211 | .303 |
| EM1 | −.226 | −.227 | EM1 | −.830 | −.557 | IUD | −.194 | .345 |
| EM2 | −.238 | .276 | EM2 | −.790 | .613 | Diaphrag | −.056 | .305 |
| SF1 | .339 | −.287 | SF1 | .870 | −.493 | Foam | .260 | .300 |
| SF2 | .166 | −.291 | SF2 | .649 | −.761 | Rhythm | .323 | −.049 |
| SM1 | .168 | −.142 | SM1 | .870 | −.493 | Abstin | .087 | −.488 |
| SM2 | −.039 | .258 | SM2 | −.221 | .975 | Withdraw | .316 | −.033 |
| AF1 | .365 | −.105 | AF1 | .982 | −.190 | Vasect | −.322 | −.178 |
| AF2 | .304 | −.147 | AF2 | .952 | −.307 | Tubal | −.350 | −.017 |
| AM1 | .159 | .394 | AM1 | .515 | .857 | Abortion | −.227 | .269 |
| AM2 | .003 | .354 | AM2 | .013 | 1.000 | Douche | .347 | .080 |
| CF1 | .145 | .094 | CF1 | .917 | .399 | Oral Sex | .117 | −.448 |
| CF2 | −.038 | −.173 | CF2 | −.314 | −.949 | Spermic | .245 | .120 |
| CM1 | −.090 | .295 | CM1 | −.415 | .910 | Hysterec | −.353 | −.105 |
| CM2 | −.091 | .213 | CM2 | −.539 | .842 | | | |

Singular Values:

| | 10.557 | 7.062 | | 4.449 | 3.613 |
|---|---|---|---|---|---|

MDPREF Latent Roots:

| | 111.448 | 49.872 | | 19.792 | 13.053 |
|---|---|---|---|---|---|

traceptive data is most clearly evident in the MDPREF analysis of row-standardized data (Figure 4.1) and in the analogous PCA (Figures 3.3, 3.4). Double standardization (Figures 3.5 and 3.6) and double-centering of data (Figure 4.1) remove the "main" effects of magnitude, allowing for a clearer examination of "interactive" factors. It is in these analyses that gender differences in the interpretation of safety, availability, and convenience become evident.

In this chapter we saw that basic structure information on row and column variables (from SVD or PCA) could be represented simultaneously in the same spatial configuration. The resulting configuration aids in the interpretation of individual differences in response patterns, the similarity of stimuli, and in "labeling" of the component factors or dimensions. We also saw how data transformations prior to analysis can remove some or all of the magnitude differences present in the data.

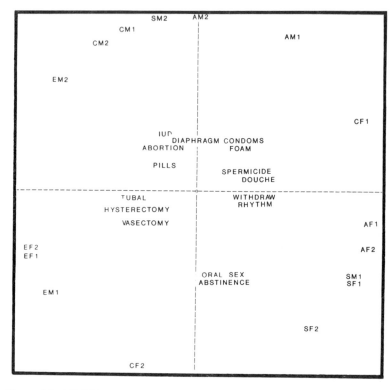

Figure 4.2. MDPREF Representation of Contraceptive Methods and Respondent Groups for Column Standardized Data

MDPREF is a dual-scaling technique that is sometimes referred to as a "vector" model, because the joint-space representation is achieved by vector-fitting. Correspondence analysis (CA), another dual-scaling technique, is a "point" model where row and column variables appear as points in the same configuration. As with MDPREF, CA achieves this principally by normalizing latent variables after factorization of the data. An important distinction between CA and MDPREF or PCA is that CA only examines interactive factors by explicitly removing magnitude effects prior to decomposition.

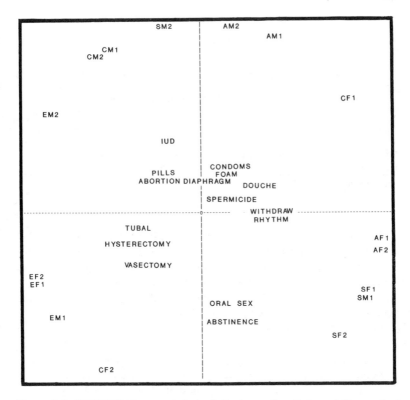

Figure 4.3. MDPREF Representation of Contraceptive Data and Respondent
Groups for Double-Centered Data

# 5. CORRESPONDENCE ANALYSIS
# OF CONTINGENCY TABLES

In this chapter we present the basic model of correspondence analysis (CA) as applied to a two-way contingency table. The emphasis is
primarily on the descriptive and exploratory aspects of the method. CA
provides a method for representing data spatially so that the results can
be visually examined for structure. For data in a typical two-dimensional contingency table both the row variables and the column variables are represented in the same geometrical space. This means that
one can examine relations not only among row or column variables but
also between row and column variables.

TABLE 5.1

1,660 Subjects Cross-Classified by
Mental Health Status and Parental Socioeconomic Status

| Mental Health Category | Parental Socioeconomic Status Stratum | | | | | |
| --- | --- | --- | --- | --- | --- | --- |
| | A | B | C | D | E | F |
| Well | 64 | 57 | 57 | 72 | 36 | 21 |
| Mild symptom formation | 94 | 94 | 105 | 141 | 97 | 71 |
| Moderate symptom formation | 58 | 54 | 65 | 77 | 54 | 54 |
| Impaired | 46 | 40 | 60 | 94 | 78 | 71 |

SOURCE: Srole et al. (1962: 213)

To illustrate the analysis we use a simple example that has been analyzed by several researchers (e.g., Gilula, 1986; Goodman, 1985; Haberman, 1974). The data are a simple cross-classification of mental health status and parental socioeconomic status from midtown Manhattan (Srole et al., 1962: 213). The data in Table 5.1 are reconstructed from percentages given in the original source.

In Table 5.1 the subjects'

SES [socioeconomic status] origins are distributed among six strata according to composite scores derived from their fathers' schooling and occupational level. With the SES-origin strata designated A through F in a sequence from highest to lowest position . . . [the table] arranges the Midtown sample adults in each status as they are distributed on the gradient classification of mental health assigned by the study psychiatrists. (Srole et al., 1962: 212-213)

An informal examination of the data in Table 5.1 reveals an apparent relation between mental health and parental socioeconomic status. There are three times as many "well" subjects among A (high) status as F (low) status, whereas there are almost twice as many "impaired" subjects among F status as A status. Questions we might ask of the data include: (1) Is the apparent relationship statistically significant? (2) Is the apparent relationship continuous, that is, more or less equal among status groups? (3) Are the categories ordered and fairly equally spaced? (4) Are some pairs of categories so similar that they should be combined?

The first question, namely, is the relationship significant, can be answered by use of the traditional Pearson Chi-square statistic for the independence model. For this data the Chi-square [$\chi^2(15) = 45.98$] is

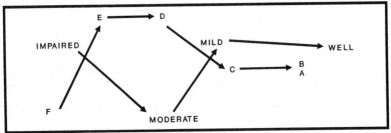

Figure 5.1. Plot of Optimal Scores for Srole Data

significant beyond the .001 level indicating that there is indeed significant association between the two variables.

Correspondence analysis provides a visual representation of this
association. Such a visual representation aids in the exploration of
questions 2, 3, and 4 above. It is important to point out that if the
Chi-square test had not rejected the independence model, it would not
make sense to apply correspondence analysis because there would be
no significant association to describe. Even though we may not always
formally test for independence, it should always be kept in mind that
correspondence analysis describes only deviations from independence,
whether that deviation is statistically significant or not.

The values representing a two-dimensional solution of the row and
column values obtained from correspondence analysis are plotted in
Figure 5.1. Notice that the main variability in the placement of the
points is in the horizontal or $X$ axis (the first dimension), whereas there
is much less variation in the vertical or $Y$ axis (the second dimension).

We can test whether both of the dimensions plotted in Figure 5.1 are
needed to account for the association present in the data. The one-
dimensional correspondence model consists of the first set of row and
column scores and the first singular value (and the independence model
from the marginal totals). This one-dimensional correspondence model
$[\chi^2(8) = 3.06]$ is not significant. The nonsignificant result indicates that
the first association or "interactive" factor (and the category totals)
provide an adequate fit or model of the data. Thus, a one-dimensional,
reduced-rank representation of the data is adequate. Note that a visual
examination of the results would probably lead to the same conclusion.
For illustrative purposes we have plotted two dimensions so that one
can visually see the difference in "size" of the two dimensions.

In Figure 5.1 all of the distances represent the degree of relationship: two points close together are closely related or similar and points further apart are less closely related or dissimilar. For example the status categories A and B are very close together indicating that there is very little distinction between these categories and they relate to the mental health categories in similar ways. The fact that the "well" category is closer to A/B than to E or F represents the fact that "well" and A/B co-occur more often than do "well" and E and F.

Note that points indicating the row and column categories are ordered as we would expect them to be. Moving across the first dimension, the mental health categories progress from "impaired" to "well" and are quite evenly spaced except that the middle two points, "moderate" + "mild," are quite similar. The socioeconomic status points are also fairly evenly spaced along the horizontal axis with two exceptions: (1) A and B are almost superimposed and (2) C and D are fairly close. We turn, now, to the numerical results underlying Figure 5.1.

Recall that the basic structure of a matrix can be represented as sets of latent variables or vectors representing the underlying components of the original rows and columns in a data matrix. Correspondence analysis always begins with a "square-root" transformation that divides each row by the square root of the row total and each column by the square root of the column total. The transformed data are then factored into their basic structure with the singular value decomposition (SVD). The U and V vectors from the SVD analysis are then rescaled into the row and column scores. We will refer to the rescaled components or latent variables as *optimal scores*. In the literature they are also referred to as *canonical scores* or *canonical variates* of the row and column variables. The *singular values* or weights are, in this case, also *canonical correlations*. The optimal scores are coordinates for the data points in normalized Euclidean space. Multiplication of these scores by their corresponding singular values or canonical correlations stretches or weights the configuration so that relative importance of the dimensions can be visualized.

The data transformation in correspondence analysis that precedes the singular value decomposition removes differences in magnitude among row and column totals, leaving the association or "interaction." It is conceptually similar to subtracting out the Chi-squared expected cell values from the observed cell values. This transformation has the consequence of setting the first set of row and column scores, as well as the first singular value, to one. This "first" factor or dimension is

TABLE 5.2

CA Results for Figure 5.1

| | Row Scores | | Singular Values | | | Column Scores | |
|---|---|---|---|---|---|---|---|
| | Dim 1 | Dim 2 | Dim 1 | Dim 2 | | Dim 1 | Dim 2 |
| Well | .646 | .063 | .161 | .037 | A | .450 | −.100 |
| Mild | .074 | .123 | | | B | .461 | −.060 |
| Mod. | −.035 | −.363 | | | C | .147 | −.115 |
| Imp. | −.591 | .098 | | | D | −.022 | .218 |
| | | | | | E | −.412 | .226 |
| | | | | | F | −.716 | −.322 |

sometimes called the "trivial factor" because it is a constant and hence contains no information. The trivial factor results when frequencies of the marginal categories are made equal. The maximum number of dimensions in correspondence analysis is one less than the rank of the matrix (in the present example, 4 − 1 = 3) because the trivial dimension is ignored.

The similarity of A and B can be seen in their unweighted scores in Table 5.2. Although not quite as close, C and D are also similar. Among the row scores the categories "mild" and "moderate" are similar. These figures reinforce the visual representation and suggest that we should form a new table that combines A and B, C and D, and "mild" and "moderate." The combining of these items would produce more evenly spaced categories. Even though we do not pursue the idea in this monograph, the collapsing of tables is a frequently recommended procedure resulting in clearer results and little loss of information (Gilula, 1986; Gilula and Haberman, 1986; Goodman, 1979, 1981). We present the condensed data in Table 5.3.

## The Mechanics of Correspondence Analysis

We present the details of how to analyze data arranged as a cross-classified contingency table both symbolically and numerically using the condensed data. In this example the units of analysis under consideration are people. The units are categorized on each of the two variables and entered into the table. We can denote this matrix as an array of frequencies, $F_{ij}$, with entries $f_{ij}$ or as a matrix $\mathbf{F}$. Correspondence analysis begins with a normalization of the data that divides each row entry by the square root of the product of corresponding row and column totals. In algebra this corresponds to

TABLE 5.3

Condensed Data From Table 5.1

| Mental Health Category | Parental Socioeconomic Status Stratum | | | | |
|---|---|---|---|---|---|
| | A + B | C + D | E | F | Total |
| Well | 121 | 129 | 36 | 21 | 307 |
| Mild + moderate | 300 | 388 | 151 | 125 | 964 |
| Impaired | 86 | 154 | 78 | 71 | 389 |
| Total | 507 | 671 | 265 | 217 | 1660 |

$$h_{ij} = f_{ij} / \sqrt{f_{i.} f_{.j}} \qquad [5.1]$$

where $h_{ij}$ is the entry for a given cell and the matrix **H** contains the transformed data, $f_{ij}$ is the original cell frequency, $f_{i.}$ is the total count for row $i$, and $f_{.j}$ is the total count in column $j$. In matrix notation it may be written as

$$\mathbf{H} = \mathbf{S}^{-1/2} \mathbf{F} \mathbf{C}^{-1/2} \qquad [5.2]$$

where $\mathbf{S}^{-1/2}$ and $\mathbf{C}^{-1/2}$ are diagonal matrices whose entries consist of reciprocals of the square root of the row marginal totals and column marginal totals, respectively. Values for the transformed, condensed data are given in Table 5.4. The value of .30670 in the first row and first column is obtained from Table 5.3, $.30670 = 121/\sqrt{307 \times 507}$.

The second step finds the basic structure of the normalized matrix **H** using SVD. This produces "summary" row and column vectors (**U** and **V** vectors of **H**) and a diagonal matrix of singular values (**d** values of **H**). The first singular value is always one and the successive values constitute singular values or canonical correlations. These values for the normalized matrix **H** are given in Table 5.5.

The final step is to rescale the row (**U**) and column (**V**) vectors to obtain the optimal or canonical scores. The calculated values are given in Table 5.6. The row (**X**) and column (**Y**) optimal or canonical scores are obtained from the row (**U**) and column (**V**) latent variables with the following rescaling formulas:

$$X_i = U_i \sqrt{f_{..} / f_{i.}} \qquad [5.3]$$

$$Y_j = V_j \sqrt{f_{..} / f_{.j}} \qquad [5.4]$$

TABLE 5.4

Normalized Data Derived From Table 5.3

| | Parental Socioeconomic Status Stratum | | | |
| Mental Health Category | A + B | C + D | E | F |
|---|---|---|---|---|
| Well | .30670 | .28422 | .12621 | .08136 |
| Mild + moderate | .42912 | .48243 | .29876 | .27330 |
| Impaired | .19365 | .30143 | .24294 | .24437 |

TABLE 5.5

Basic Structure of Normalized Data in Table 5.4

| | Row Vectors (U) | | | | Column Vectors (V) | | |
| | Dim 0 | Dim 1 | Dim 2 | | Dim 0 | Dim 1 | Dim 2 |
|---|---|---|---|---|---|---|---|
| Well | .430 | .702 | −.568 | A + B | .553 | .638 | .455 |
| Mild + moderate | .762 | .055 | .645 | C + D | .636 | .075 | −.512 |
| Impaired | .484 | −.710 | −.511 | E | .399 | −.425 | −.373 |
| | | | | F | .362 | −.638 | .633 |
| Singular Values | | | | | | | |
| (R) | 1.000 | .159 | .008 | | 1.000 | .159 | .008 |

TABLE 5.6

Optimal scores calculated from data in Table 5.5

| | Row Optimal Scores (X) | | | | Column Optimal Scores (Y) | | |
| | Dim 0 | Dim 1 | Dim 2 | | Dim 0 | Dim 1 | Dim 2 |
|---|---|---|---|---|---|---|---|
| Well | 1.000 | 1.632 | −1.321 | A + B | 1.000 | 1.154 | .805 |
| Mild + moderate | 1.000 | .073 | .847 | C + D | 1.000 | .119 | −.805 |
| Impaired | 1.000 | −1.467 | −1.056 | E | 1.000 | −1.063 | −.935 |
| | | | | F | 1.000 | −1.765 | 1.750 |

Notice that the first scores are all 1.000. This is always true and serves as a check on the calculations. It corresponds to the independence model of Chi-square expected values. This is the factor that is frequently referred to as the "trivial factor" and is ignored in subsequent analysis. It corresponds with the first singular value, which is also 1.000. The first trivial optimal column score is calculated from the V value (Table 5.5) and the marginal totals (Table 5.3). Thus denoting the trivial score by $Y_0$, $Y_0 = .553\sqrt{1660/507}$, which gives .9999, within rounding error of 1.000.

Thus three steps are necessary for a correspondence analysis. First, the raw frequencies $(f_{ij})$ are normalized by the square-root transformation $(h_{ij})$. Second, the normalized matrix is decomposed with SVD into its basic structure, that is, $\mathbf{H} = \mathbf{U}d\mathbf{V}^T$. Third, the row and column vectors, $\mathbf{U}$ and $\mathbf{V}$, are rescaled to obtain the optimal scores or canonical variates.

These optimal or canonical scores are those most frequently quoted in the literature. It is very important to remember that they are unweighted and thus assume that each dimension is equally important, that is, they are weighted the same. When we desire to compare scores within and between rows and columns and between and within various dimensions we must take a final step and weight the scores as a function of the size of the singular values. The numbers reported in Table 5.2 are the (nontrivial) weighted values, obtained by multiplying the unweighted values by the square root of the corresponding singular values, the most common practice, and plotted in Figure 5.1. Other weighting methods have been suggested in the literature (Carroll, Green, and Schaffer, 1986).

## The Reconstruction of Expected and Observed Data

One of the important characteristics of correspondence analysis is that we can reconstruct the expected values of the data, depending on how many dimensions of optimal scores and singular values are utilized, as was shown in Chapter 2. The fundamental formula involved for reconstructing the frequencies for each cell of the original contingency table is

$$f_{ij} = \frac{f_{i\cdot} f_{\cdot j}}{f_{\cdot\cdot}} \left( 1.00 + \sum R_k X_k Y_k \right) \qquad [5.5]$$

where the subscript $k$ refers to the number of dimensions (beyond the trivial factor denoted by the 1.00 preceding the $\Sigma$ in formula 5.5) to be used in the reconstruction; $X$ and $Y$ are the row and component vectors, respectively; and $R$ refers to the singular values. Because the maximum rank of the matrix is three in this case, the maximum number of dimensions, $k$, is two. Two dimensions will reconstruct the original data exactly. In effect, the values in each cell are being reconstructed from three components: (1) the $\chi^2$ expected values associated with the trivial factor and first singular value, $R_0$, (2) the component associated with the first canonical correlation, $R_1$, and (3) the component associated with the second canonical correlation, $R_2$. Note that the first canonical correlation is the second singular value. The independence model consists of the first or zero-order component; a one-dimensional solution includes the independence model (trivial factor) and the component associated with the first; and a two-dimensional solution includes all three components (0, 1, 2).

Another way to picture this is to break the formula into its three components as follows:

$$f_{ij} = \frac{f_i.f_{.j}}{f_{..}}(1.0) + \frac{f_i.f_{.j}}{f_{..}}R_1 X_1 Y_1 + \frac{f_i.f_{.j}}{f_{..}}R_2 X_2 Y_2 \qquad [5.6]$$

The original data are reconstructed by summing the three components. The expected numbers for the independence model consists of the values obtained from the first component only. Note that the (1.0) at the end of the first component is $R_0$. The expected numbers for a one-dimensional correspondence analysis would be the sum of the first two components because the reconstruction is cumulative.

In the example of mental health and socioeconomic status each dimension or a cumulation of dimensions can be used to reconstruct the original data. To do this we use a detailed numerical example in Table 5.7. Focusing on the upper left-hand cell in Table 5.7, we can substitute numbers obtained from Tables 5.3 and 5.6 into formula 5.6.

$$f_{11} = \frac{f_1.f_{.1}}{f_{..}}(1) + \frac{f_1.f_{.1}}{f_{..}}R_1 X_1 Y_1 + \frac{f_1.f_{.1}}{f_{..}}R_2 X_2 Y_2$$

$$= \frac{307 \times 507}{1660}(1) + \frac{307 \times 507}{1660}0.1589 \times 1.632 \times 1.154$$

$$+ \frac{307 \times 507}{1660}0.0083 \times -1.321 \times 0.805$$

$$= 93.764 + 28.060 + -.828$$

$$= 120.997$$

Here, 93.764 is the contribution of the trivial factor or marginal totals: It is the Chi-square expected value. The contribution of the first

TABLE 5.7

Reconstruction of Original Data of Table 5.3

| Mental Health Category | A + B | C + D | E | F | Row Scores |
|---|---|---|---|---|---|
| | *Parental Socioeconomic Status Stratum* | | | | |
| **Well** | | | | | |
| Dim 0 | 93.764 | 124.095 | 49.009 | 40.132 | 1.000 |
| Dim 1 | 28.060 | 3.814 | −13.510 | −18.364 | 1.632 |
| Dim 2 | −.828 | 1.092 | .500 | .766 | −1.321 |
| Total | 120.997 | 129.000 | 36.000 | 21.000 | |
| **Mild + moderate** | | | | | |
| Dim 0 | 294.427 | 389.665 | 153.892 | 126.017 | 1.000 |
| Dim 1 | 3.913 | .532 | −1.885 | −2.562 | .073 |
| Dim 2 | 1.660 | −2.197 | −1.007 | 1.545 | .847 |
| Total | 300.000 | 388.000 | 151.000 | 125.000 | |
| **Impaired** | | | | | |
| Dim 0 | 118.809 | 157.240 | 62.099 | 50.851 | 1.000 |
| Dim 1 | −31.974 | −4.345 | 15.394 | 20.926 | −1.467 |
| Dim 2 | −.835 | 1.105 | .507 | −.777 | −1.056 |
| Total | 86.000 | 154.000 | 78.000 | 71.000 | |
| **Column scores** | | | | | |
| Dim 0 | 1.000 | 1.000 | 1.000 | 1.000 | |
| Dim 1 | 1.154 | .119 | −1.063 | −1.765 | |
| Dim 2 | .805 | −.805 | −.935 | 1.750 | |

Singular values are $R_0$ = 1.000, $R_1$ = .1589, $R_2$ = .0083

nontrivial factor is 28.060. Thus, in a one-dimensional estimate of the data, the first cell in the table would be 121.824 (93.764 + 28.060). A two-dimensional estimate of that cell is 121 (93.764 + 28.060 − .828 = 120.997). Note that the unweighted scores are used for this reconstruction. To get any element of the table one simply forms the product of the row score, the column score, and the singular value and multiplies the result by the expected value, that is, $f_i . f_{.j}/f_{..}$, in formula 5.5 above.

Because correspondence analysis only analyzes the association in contingency tables one should always determine that the independence model of no association can be rejected. In this example a test of the independence model $[\chi^2(6) = 42.04]$ is significant beyond the .001 level, indicating that the independence model does not account for the data very well. In fact, there is a precise mathematical relation between correspondence analysis and Chi-square:

TABLE 5.8

Table Showing the Different Ways of Viewing the
Singular Values of the Condensed Srole Data

| Factor or Dimension | Singular Value | Squared Singular Values | Percent Total | Percent Inertia | Chi-Squared |
|---|---|---|---|---|---|
| Trivial | 1.0000 | 1.00000 | .9753 | | |
| 1 | .1589 | .02525 | .0246 | .9972 | 41.916 |
| 2 | .0083 | .000007 | .00007 | .0028 | .120 |
| Totals | 1.1672 | 1.02532 | 1.0000 | 1.0000 | 42.036 |

$\chi^2 / n$ = Sum of Squared Singular Values (excluding Trivial)

Thus $42.036 / 1660 = .02532 = .1589^2 + .0083^2$

$$\frac{\chi^2}{n} = \sum R_i^2 \qquad \text{(excluding } R_0, \text{ the trivial factor)} \qquad [5.7]$$

where $n$ is the sum of all frequencies in the original data. Thus the sum of the squared canonical correlations is equivalent to the degree of association present in the data.

As we saw in the chapters on PCA and MDPREF, goodness-of-fit can be estimated with the singular values. Here, the singular values are squared, to parallel eigenvalues. Table 5.8 shows the relevant data and calculations for the condensed Srole data. The first canonical correlation accounts for virtually all (99.7%) of the association (next to last column in Table 5.8). Greenacre (1984) and other followers of Benzecri (1969) call the association "inertia" and examine the proportion of "inertia" accounted for by each of the singular values. This terminology is used and reported by BMDP (Dixon, Brown, Engelman, Hill, and Jennrich, 1988).

We recommend examination of all the singular values including the trivial one to get an overall perspective of the data. In the present case it reminds us that although 99.7% of the association is accounted for by the first canonical factor, the independence model (row and column "main" effects) accounts for almost 97.5% of the total variability in the data.

In order to test whether a one-dimensional model adequately accounts for the data we create a one-dimensional estimate of the data with formula 5.5. This is equivalent to summing the first two numbers in each cell in Table 5.7; for example, 93.764 + 28.060 = 121.824. This estimate can serve as a theoretical expected value and a Chi-square test can be used to compare the "estimated data" with the actual or observed data. Such a test produces a nonsignificant result indicating a very good fit. Thus, the second dimension is not necessary to account adequately for the data.

## Another Perspective:
## The Case Approach with Indicator Variables

We have presented a simple example of correspondence analysis and shown the detailed steps in carrying out an analysis using cross-classified data. There are many useful variations and elaborations possible on the model that make it a rich and adaptable tool in a wide variety of contexts. We now repeat the analysis using the condensed data just considered, but with a new perspective. The new perspective allows us to arrive at the same answers using a different approach and arrangement of the basic data.

The data in Table 5.3 can be rearranged into a very large binary (1 if a subject belongs to a category, 0 otherwise) matrix of 1660 rows (each representing a subject) and 7 columns (three representing the row variables and four representing column variables). In such an array each row would sum to exactly 2 because each subject can belong to only one category of each variable.

With all 1660 observations there would be 121 identical rows corresponding to the cell in Table 5.3 where "well" and A + B intersect, 71 rows for the cell in Table 5.3 where "impaired" and F intersect, and so on for each of the other cells. This creates an alternative display of exactly the same data. It is possible to carry out a correspondence analysis on this data as well and except for some slight rescaling the results parallel the previous analysis.

Nishisato and Sheu (1980) have shown that the results are invariant in such a table if identical rows are simply added together and the 1's replaced by the sum or number of identical rows. Thus in the above example, the first 121 rows could be represented by one row with 121 in place of the 1's. Following the same procedure we can represent the data in Table 5.3 with 12 rows as shown in Table 5.9.

The optimal scores found at the bottom of the table are exactly the same as those reported for the corresponding unweighted scores for the same data reported in Table 5.6 and again in Table 5.7. The singular

TABLE 5.9

Tallied Indicator Variable With Correspondence Analysis Results

| | Mental Health Category | | | Parental Socioeconomic Status | | | | Row Scores |
| | Well | Mild + Mod | Impaired | A + B | C + D | E | F | (Dim 1) |
|---|---|---|---|---|---|---|---|---|
| Cell | | | | | | | | |
| 11 | 121 | 0 | 0 | 121 | 0 | 0 | 0 | 1.830 |
| 21 | 0 | 300 | 0 | 300 | 0 | 0 | 0 | .806 |
| 31 | 0 | 0 | 86 | 86 | 0 | 0 | 0 | −.206 |
| 12 | 129 | 0 | 0 | 0 | 129 | 0 | 0 | 1.150 |
| 22 | 0 | 388 | 0 | 0 | 388 | 0 | 0 | .126 |
| 32 | 0 | 0 | 154 | 0 | 154 | 0 | 0 | −.886 |
| 13 | 36 | 0 | 0 | 0 | 0 | 36 | 0 | .374 |
| 23 | 0 | 151 | 0 | 0 | 0 | 151 | 0 | −.651 |
| 33 | 0 | 0 | 78 | 0 | 0 | 78 | 0 | −1.662 |
| 14 | 21 | 0 | 0 | 0 | 0 | 0 | 21 | −.087 |
| 24 | 0 | 125 | 0 | 0 | 0 | 0 | 125 | −1.112 |
| 34 | 0 | 0 | 71 | 0 | 0 | 0 | 71 | −2.123 |

Column Scores

| | | | | | | | |
|---|---|---|---|---|---|---|---|
| Dim 1 | 1.632 | .073 | −1.467 | 1.154 | .119 | −1.063 | −1.765 |
| Dim 2 | −1.321 | .847 | −1.056 | .805 | −.805 | −.935 | 1.750 |

Sinqular values are $R_0 = 1.0000$, $R_1 = .7612$, $R_2 = .7100$

values, on the other hand, appear to be different; however, they are linked by a simple formula as follows:

$$R_C^2 = (2R_I^2 - 1)^2 \qquad [5.8]$$

where $R_C$ is the singular value from the contingency table analysis and $R_I$ is the singular value from the indicator matrix analysis. For example, the first nontrivial singular value (the first canonical correlation, $R_1$) works out as follows:

$$.1589^2 = [(2 \times .7612^2) - 1]^2$$

Equation 5.8 suggests that $R_I^2$ should be equal to or greater than .5. This is only true for the $R_I^2$'s that correspond to the $R_C^2$'s from the analysis of the contingency table format. There are more solutions to the indicator variable format because the rank of the matrix is higher and requires more information for its complete reconstruction. An important point is that the analysis of the indicator variable format

68

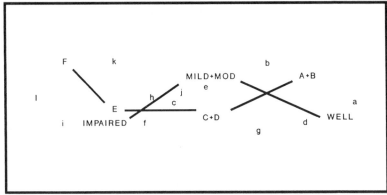

Figure 5.2. Plot of Optimal Scores of Condensed Version of Srole Data

corresponds precisely with the contingency table analysis up to the rank of the contingency table, even though it has additional singular values and optimal scores that can be ignored for our purposes.

The indicator variable format also has the interesting advantage of showing the relationship of each type of subject, as represented in the 12 cells of the contingency table, to each other and to the various categories of the two variables. The first set of row scores are shown in Table 5.9. For illustration we plot the first two sets of row and column scores in Figure 5.2. We have plotted the scores weighted by the square root of the singular values in Table 5.6, namely, $\sqrt{.1589}$ and $\sqrt{.0083}$. This makes them exactly parallel to the corresponding points plotted in Figure 5.1.

Notice that the mental health categories and the parental socioeconomic status categories are evenly spaced and that we can see where each type of subject occurs relative to the categories. Although it is beyond the scope of this monograph, it is interesting to note that Goodman (1979) has developed models for testing if the categories are evenly spaced. For this example he finds that the condensed data (Table 5.3) fit the hypothesis of equally spaced categories very well $[\chi^2(5) = 1.27]$.

One of the many important and interesting properties of correspondence analysis is the fact that the optimal scores for the rows of the indicator variable format can be calculated directly from the contingency table results. Note that any row of the indicator matrix corresponds to some specific cell of the contingency table. Thus by calculating a score for a cell in the contingency table we get a score for a row of the indicator matrix. Nishisato and Sheu (1980: 470) give the following formula for the optimal score of any cell $f_{ij}$ of the contingency table $F$ as follows:

$$X_{ij} = \frac{Y_{1i} + Y_{2j}}{\sqrt{2(R_C^2 + 1)}} \qquad [5.9]$$

where the first subscripts on the $Y$'s represent the row (1) and column (2) variables and the second subscripts the categories, and $R_C$ is the singular value from the contingency table calculations.

We can illustrate this numerically from the numbers given in Table 5.6 and recall that the first singular value $R_{C1} = .1589$. We can calculate the optimal score for the first row as follows:

$$X_{11} = \frac{1.632 + 1.154}{\sqrt{2(.159 + 1)}}$$

$$= \frac{2.786}{\sqrt{2.318}}$$

$$= 1.830$$

which is the same as shown for row one in Table 5.9, which corresponds to the first row and first column cell in Table 5.3. In case we already knew or wanted to calculate $R_1$ (from $R_C$) for the indicator variable format, it is interesting to note that the optimal score for a subject can be calculated as the average of the optimal scores the categories involved, divided by $R_1$. In this instance we have 2.786/1.522 = 1.830. This holds for any number of variables that have been put into indicator format.

For the analysis in the contingency format the $X$ and $Y$ optimal scores can always be calculated in terms of each other. The relevant formulas are given by Kendall and Stuart (1961: 571):

$$Y_j = \frac{1}{R_i f_{\cdot j}} \sum_i f_{ij} X_i \qquad [5.10]$$

$$X_i = \frac{1}{R_i f_{i \cdot}} \sum_j f_{ij} Y_j \qquad [5.11]$$

We can calculate $Y_1$ to illustrate how this works in numerical terms using figures from Tables 5.3 and 5.6,

$$Y_1 = \frac{1}{.159 \times 507}[(121 \times 1.632) + (300 \times .073) + (86 \times -1.467)]$$

$$= \frac{1}{80.563(92.989)}$$

$$= 1.154$$

This completes our description of simple correspondence analysis as applied to a basic contingency table of cross-classified frequency counts and the associated indicator matrix. We will now turn to some examples of various extensions and generalizations of this basic model and then to multiway models of multiple correspondence analysis.

# 6. CORRESPONDENCE ANALYSIS
# OF NONFREQUENCY DATA

The analysis presented in the last chapter has intimate statistical relations to a number of other classical statistical procedures including *canonical correlation,* analysis of variance, discriminant analysis, and *association* models. Even though detailed inferential considerations are beyond the purposes of this monograph it is important to indicate that recent years have seen great advances in the field. Those interested in pursuing the topic might begin with Goodman (1985), Gilula and Haberman (1986), Wasserman (1988), and Wasserman and Faust (1989).

Correspondence analysis (CA) provides a very close approximation to the results of the other procedures, including those that use maximum likelihood methods. In fact, the singular value decomposition approach used throughout this monograph as well as in the BMDP package (Dixon, Brown, Engelman, Hill, and Jennrich, 1988) is a least squares solution rather than a maximum likelihood one. In practice it is exceedingly rare for the methods to give answers that are noticeably different.

Even though CA is, and canonical analysis originally was, derived from two-way frequency tables they may be usefully extended, for descriptive purposes, to many other kinds of data. When applied to nonfrequency data, such as rank-order data, or intensity data like the color cone example, or any of a variety of proximity indices, CA provides an excellent *description* of the data. CA can be applied directly to any frequency-type data where cells indicate a tabulated total, for example, the number of positive responses, a total dollar amount, a total score, or even a total measured amount as in the receptor cone example. As a purely descriptive device we may extend it to various kinds of proximity data as in the example of distance between cities to be described below or any other kind of pseudo-frequency data. When CA is generalized beyond strict frequency data a few important restrictions are to be noted.

When using CA in a purely descriptive and exploratory manner with data other than strict frequency data the restrictions are very important. We discuss five of these conditions in the following paragraphs and then provide illustrative examples of the descriptive use of CA for nonfrequency data. Keeping these precautions in mind it is possible to apply CA to a great many kinds of data.

First, inferential tests such as Chi-square are not valid when the cell values are not frequencies (nor when expected frequencies are too low). CA still may be useful as a descriptive device for obtaining a notion of the structure of the data. Nevertheless, it is a good idea to use some descriptive measure of how well the data are fit by the representation even though formal inference may not be appropriate. Goodness-of-fit can be estimated from the squared singular values. Or, one could reconstruct the expected values for a $k$-dimensional representation of the data and compute a correlation between the expected values and the data. This latter approach is used in the kinship example discussed in Chapter 8. More exotic tests such as "bootstrapping" are also sometimes used (Greenacre, 1984: 293).

Second, the data must be in the form of "similarities." If rank-order data are to be analyzed this means that the preferred choice should be the *largest* number rather than the more common use of one for first choice. If the data are in the form of distances, for example the distances between cities, this should be reflected by subtracting the distances from a number larger than the largest distance.

Third, when analyzing square matrices in which the items in the rows are the same as the items in the columns, it is critical that the diagonal values have a large positive value. This kind of data arises frequently in social network studies where the matrix might be observations of interactions or a set of people might rank each other on how well they like each other. The diagonal values represent how often individuals were observed or how well individuals liked themselves and might otherwise have been left blank or assigned the value of zero. In analyzing such data with CA it is very important that the diagonal cells are assigned large positive values (normally equal to or one larger than the largest value in the off-diagonal cells).

Fourth, all values in the data matrix must be positive (zeros are acceptable) and all row and column totals must be greater than zero. If any of the numbers in the table are negative the first singular value will not be one, and the results will be invalid and misleading. The general rule is to be able to imagine that the data are "quasi-" or "pseudo-frequencies." For example, rank-order data may be thought of as the number of choices received by each item, and similarity data (from triadic comparisons or pile sorts of stimuli) may be thought of as the number of times a pair of items is classified as similar. The descriptive use of CA for such data can be useful even though ordinary Chi-square inferential tests are invalid.

Finally, in the analysis of sparse matrices one should also be alert to other simple and rather obvious "defects" in the data. One possible "defect" in scarce data arises when there are two or more "disjoint" sets. This might arise, for example, if one asked new students in a high school to indicate all the students with whom they were acquainted. If the students came from different primary schools there may be no one in school A who knows anyone in school B, and vice versa. The two groups would be disjoint. The row and column scores from CA would have complementary vectors of zeros and real values. The two disjoint sets should be separated and analyzed separately.

## Correspondence Analysis of Rank-Order Data

The application of the above considerations to rank-order data reveals that CA is appropriate for the analysis of such data if we assume rank as a linear measure. We will illustrate the analysis on the contraceptive data introduced in Chapter 3. Prior to our analysis let us note how we have applied the restrictions discussed above.

First, we will apply descriptive measures of fit rather than attempting to apply Chi-square tests to decide how many dimensions are useful or necessary to describe the data adequately. Second, we note that the data are ordered as "similarity" data where the most preferred choice is the largest number. In this case each row represents the aggregation of several subjects but the principle applies to individual as well as aggregated data. We treat rank-ordered data as "quasi-frequency" data that may be seen as the amount of choice received by each item. An object that receives a rank of 15 rather than 13 receives two more units of choice.

Our treatment of rank-order data is only one of a number of ways of analyzing such data. Nishisato (1980: 120-148) has an extended treatment of alternative methods and Greenacre (1984: 169-184) has a section on doubling data in the case of ratings and preferences. Nishisato found that most of the methods give equivalent results. A comparison of the various methods, including doubling, shows that there are virtually no practical differences in the various results. The "doubling" method described by Greenacre (1984) for so-called "bipolar" rating data essentially includes both similarity and "dissimilarity" forms of the data in the analysis.

We now return to the contraceptive data (Table 3.3). Because the data have already been examined from the point of view of both PCA and MDPREF we can turn directly to the results obtained with CA. The squared singular values indicate that 91.1% of the total variance can be explained by differences in marginal totals. In the remaining 8.9% of the variance (the association or "inertia"), 60.3% can be explained with the first factor and 17.5% with the second (77.8% of the association is explained in a two-dimensional representation). We compare the spatial representation (Figure 6.1) with those presented in earlier chapters.

Notice that CA plots both the subject scores (row variables) and the contraceptive scores (column variables) in the same space. Subjects are closest to the contraceptives they ranked the highest and furthest from those they ranked the lowest. Subject groups are close together if they ranked the contraceptives similarly and are further apart if their rankings diverged from each other. Contraceptive methods are close together to the extent they received similar rankings from subject groups. The placing of both the row variables and the column variables explicitly in the same space is one of the important advantages of CA and is a great aid in interpretation of the data. Correspondence analysis of this kind is being increasingly used in studies of consumer preferences (Carroll, Green, and Schaffer, 1986) and may be viewed as another approach to multidimensional preference scaling.

If we compare the relative arrangement of contraceptive methods in Figure 6.1 with those in Figures 3.1 and 3.5 we can see that results from PCA (with column standardization) and CA are quite similar. The MDPREF results for column-standardized and double-centered data (Figures 4.2 and 4.3) also provide similar results for the general rela-

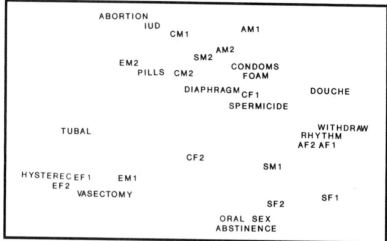

Figure 6.1. Correspondence Analysis Plot of Contraception Data From Chapter 3

tionships among contraceptive methods. Note, however, that the PCA results shown in Figure 3.4 and the MDPREF results for row-standardized data shown in Figure 4.1 diverge somewhat from the CA results.

This divergence is due to different standardizing procedures applied in each case. The "square-root" transformation used in CA has the effect of "standardizing" both row and column variables. Because, in this kind of data, column standardization has a large effect, the three results that involved column standardization are the most similar.

Some standardization techniques produce data that when analyzed by all three methods give identical results. The double standardization of both row and column variables carried out iteratively (Chapter 3) is an important and critical example. Double standardization removes differences in row and column totals and thus prevents confounding of magnitude differences with patterns of association in both PCA and MDPREF. Adding a constant to doubly-standardized data (to make all cell values positive) allows a CA analysis. PCA, MDPREF, and CA give identical (up to multiplication by a known constant) results for such data. It is instructive to note that a simple SVD of the doubly-standardized data also gives the same results.

TABLE 6.1

Similarities Among Ten U.S. Cities

| Cities | Atl. | Chi. | Den. | Hous. | L.A. | Miam. | N.Y. | S.F. | Sea. | D.C. |
|---|---|---|---|---|---|---|---|---|---|---|
| Atlanta | 2735 | 2148 | 1523 | 2034 | 799 | 2131 | 1987 | 596 | 553 | 2192 |
| Chicago | 2148 | 2735 | 1815 | 1795 | 990 | 1547 | 2022 | 877 | 998 | 2138 |
| Denver | 1523 | 1815 | 2735 | 1856 | 1904 | 1009 | 1104 | 1786 | 1714 | 1241 |
| Houston | 2034 | 1795 | 1856 | 2735 | 1361 | 1767 | 1315 | 1090 | 844 | 1515 |
| Los Angeles | 799 | 990 | 1904 | 1361 | 2735 | 396 | 284 | 2388 | 1776 | 435 |
| Miami | 2131 | 1547 | 1009 | 1767 | 396 | 2735 | 1643 | 141 | 1 | 1812 |
| New York | 1987 | 2022 | 1104 | 1315 | 284 | 1643 | 2735 | 164 | 327 | 2530 |
| San Francisco | 596 | 877 | 1786 | 1090 | 2388 | 141 | 164 | 2735 | 2057 | 293 |
| Seattle | 553 | 998 | 1714 | 844 | 1776 | 1 | 327 | 2057 | 2735 | 406 |
| Washington D.C. | 2192 | 2138 | 1241 | 1515 | 435 | 1812 | 2530 | 293 | 406 | 2735 |

## Correspondence Analysis of Proximities

We turn now to another example of generalizing CA beyond strict frequency data. In this case we see how to transform distance data into similarity data to obtain a spatial representation of the position of cities. In an earlier volume, Kruskal and Wish (1978: 7-9) illustrate an application of multidimensional scaling in finding the relative position among cities from a table of distances among cities.

In order to apply correspondence analysis to such data we must first transform the data into "quasi-frequencies" or similarity data by subtracting them from a number larger than the largest value in the table. Because the largest distance (from Miami to Seattle) is 2734 we subtract all distances in the table from 2735. Because the number zero was originally on the diagonal this automatically sets the value of each diagonal cell at 2735. The results are shown in Table 6.1.

In the transformed data the cities that are closest together have the largest numbers, hence, they form a similarity matrix. Because each city is obviously closer to itself than to any other city the diagonal cell has the largest entry. It is the transformed data that are analyzed with correspondence analysis. Because the matrix is symmetric the row and column scores are equal to each other. Figure 6.2 shows a plot of the first two sets of weighted scores.

The cities seem to be placed in their correct relative positions. We can describe the degree of fit by correlating the values reconstructed from the first two row scores with the original airline distances given

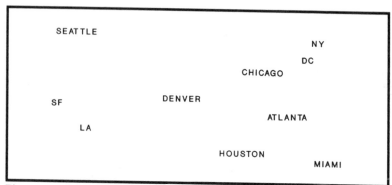

Figure 6.2. Correspondence Analysis Plot of Scores for Outline Distance Between Cities

in Table 6.1. The correlation is .95 which indicates a close fit to the original data. This means that we can place a good deal of confidence in the representation given by Figure 6.2 even though we cannot actually use correspondence analysis for inferential purposes in this case.

## 7. ORDINATION, SERIATION, AND GUTTMAN SCALING

One reason that CA is gaining popularity at such a rapid rate is that it provides a rather simple solution to a number of classical research questions. One of these problems is how best to order a series of objects based upon a given series of characteristics. This is illustrated in almost pure form in the problem of chronological seriation in archaeology. In the field of ecology, which has made extensive use of CA, the term "ordination" rather than "seriation" is used (see, e.g., Digby and Kempton, 1987). We will examine a sample problem of archaeological seriation in the first section of this chapter and then extend the same logic to another social science problem involving Guttman scaling.

The underlying assumption of chronological seriation is based on the similarities among the assemblages of artifacts found at the sites under consideration. It is assumed that each type of artifact "originates at a given time at a given place, is made in gradually increasing numbers as time goes on, then decreases in popularity until it becomes forgotten, never to recur in an identical form" (Brainerd, 1951: 304). Assume that

TABLE 7.1

Frequencies of Pottery Type (Columns) for Each of Nine Levels
From the Site Tepe Sabz (Rows)

| Pottery Type Code Number[a] | | | | | | | | | | | | | | | | |
|---|---|---|---|---|---|---|---|---|---|---|---|---|---|---|---|---|
| 15 | 16 | 17 | 18 | 19 | 20 | 21 | 22 | 23 | 24 | 25 | 28 | 29 | 31 | 32 | 35 | 36 |
| 53 | 1 | 5 | 47 | 0 | 25 | 5 | 29 | 8 | 0 | 45 | 0 | 0 | 7 | 2 | 1 | 2 |
| 105 | 10 | 6 | 80 | 0 | 27 | 4 | 18 | 40 | 0 | 78 | 0 | 1 | 15 | 2 | 0 | 1 |
| 55 | 47 | 2 | 32 | 13 | 16 | 2 | 20 | 81 | 0 | 80 | 2 | 0 | 11 | 6 | 0 | 4 |
| 4 | 6 | 3 | 2 | 10 | 1 | 1 | 0 | 20 | 2 | 13 | 0 | 0 | 1 | 3 | 1 | 1 |
| 23 | 51 | 12 | 16 | 33 | 7 | 2 | 2 | 156 | 0 | 131 | 1 | 0 | 3 | 4 | 4 | 1 |
| 12 | 20 | 6 | 10 | 36 | 12 | 3 | 0 | 132 | 19 | 147 | 2 | 1 | 5 | 7 | 9 | 2 |
| 6 | 5 | 2 | 2 | 4 | 3 | 2 | 0 | 127 | 118 | 150 | 7 | 9 | 5 | 2 | 4 | 1 |
| 1 | 2 | 0 | 1 | 2 | 1 | 1 | 1 | 101 | 37 | 88 | 13 | 2 | 10 | 0 | 8 | 0 |
| 0 | 2 | 0 | 0 | 0 | 1 | 1 | 0 | 55 | 31 | 48 | 13 | 0 | 3 | 0 | 6 | 0 |

a. These are various "Susiana Black-on-Buff" Deh Luran pottery types listed in Hole and Shaw (1967, p. 98). Note that we have dropped pottery types 14, 26, 27, 30, 33, and 34 because of low frequencies. The rows are sites and levels of sites as described in the text.

each site is characterized by a unique profile of frequencies of artifact types at any given time. It would follow that sites close together in time would have profiles very similar to each other. Sites further apart in time should be less similar to each other while the most dissimilar sites should be at the start and finish of the sequence.

CA provides an optimal solution to the problem of ordering both the row items and the column items from one extreme to the other (e.g., early to late, low to high socioeconomic class, young to old) with adjacent items being most similar to each other.

In order to illustrate the application to archaeological data we use an example from Hole and Shaw (1967) whose book, *Computer Analysis of Chronological Seriation,* is a nice introduction to seriation even though the authors were unaware of CA. Table 7.1 presents a subset of data from their work showing the distribution of a number of pottery types by site and level within sites (Hole and Shaw, 1967: 99). With the exception of row six, each of the rows represent a specific stratigraphic level within a single site called Tepe Sabz in the region of Deh Luran in Khuzistan (see Hole and Shaw, 1967: 51-54, for details). Three well-defined phases are subdivided into arbitrary levels. The phases are dated by radiocarbon dating, whereas the levels within phases cannot be reliably dated. The sixth row in the table was from a nearby site and "is included to see how it seriates with reference to the master sequence" (Hole and Shaw, 1967: 52). The relevant data may be summarized as follows:

```
Row 1. 5500-5000 B.C. Khazineh phase designated as KHA2
Row 2. 5500-5000 B.C. Khazineh phase designated as KHA1
Row 3. 5000-4500 B.C. Mahmeh  phase designated as MEH3
Row 4. 5000-4500 B.C. Mahmeh  phase designated as MEH2
Row 5. 5000-4500 B.C. Mahmeh  phase designated as MEH1
Row 6.     ?          Musiyan phase designated as MUSE
Row 7. 4000-3500 B.C. Bayat   phase designated as BAY3
Row 8. 4000-3500 B.C. Bayat   phase designated as BAY2
Row 9. 4000-3500 B.C. Bayat   phase designated as BAY1
```

We have analyzed the data as a contingency table with CA as described in Chapter 5. Figure 7.1 shows a two-dimensional representation of the data. Note that the Khazineh, Mahmeh, and Bayat phases form distinct clusters. The two-dimensional representation accounts for 94.5% of the total variance (61.1% of which is explained by differences in marginals). Because the pottery types are not meaningful to the nonspecialist we have entered them in the figure as asterisks.

## The Horseshoe Effect

Figure 7.1 illustrates a very common result in studies involving seriation and ordination, namely, that the method does not necessarily result in a straight linear sequence of sites or objects. Rather it is frequently curvilinear or pyramidal, as in this case. The curved shape sometimes resembles a horseshoe, hence the name. A good description of the effect can be found in Digby and Kempton (1987: 93-105, see also Kruskal and Wish, 1978: Appendix B) who suggest that a "single dominant gradient describing the samples will usually be detected from the ordination [seriation] diagram despite the presence of curvilinearity, particularly if near neighbors are connected" (p. 97). Notice the correspondence to the order determined by stratigraphic techniques. The exceptions are the misplacement of BAY3 and MEH2. It is highly likely that the distinctions visible among the phases are significant and stable whereas the much smaller distinctions visible within phases are not reliable and represent sampling variability and measurement error. The possible exception is the distinction between MEH3 and the latter two phases of MEH.

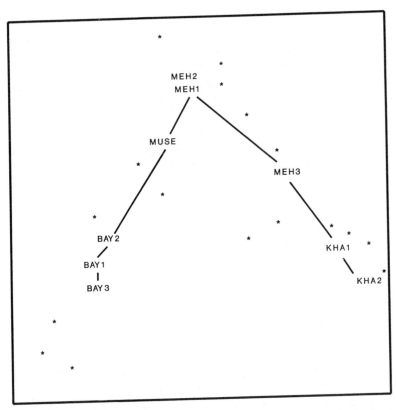

Figure 7.1. Optimal Scores Plotted to Represent Relations Among Archeological Sites

## Guttman Scaling as a Special
## Case of Correspondence Analysis

A somewhat distinctive type of unidimensional scaling known as "Guttman scaling" can be solved with CA. The aim of Guttman scaling is to order a series of objects so that the order is generally transitive. For example, Kay (1964) presented data that show a definite order of acquisition of durable consumer goods among households in a neighborhood of Papeete, French Polynesia. The objects and the order of acquisition are: primus stove, bicycle, radio, two-wheeled motor vehicle, kerosene or gas stove, refrigerator, and automobile. In general if a household has an object on the list then they also have all the objects occurring earlier on the list. If they lack any item in the list they tend not to have items later in the list. The data are shown in Table 7.2.

Note that each item is coded explicitly for both occurrence and nonoccurrence, hence the data are "doubled." The odd numbered columns correspond to Kay's (1964) coding and the even numbered columns correspond to not having the item. This has the effect of creating a multiway "indicator" matrix with equal row totals. This is a direct generalization of the indicator matrix format discussed in Chapter 5. This generalization to multiway "indicator" matrices has many important uses and can be extended to multiple choice questions or items in a straightforward manner.

When we apply CA to an indicator matrix as shown in Table 7.2 we obtain the row and column optimal scores. Figure 7.2 again shows the horseshoe effect characteristic of ordered data. The consumer items are in the same order as in the original study (Kay, 1964: 161).

Table 7.3 shows the households rearranged according to the row optimal scores. We have put extra spacing between the gaps in scores as determined by numerical examination. The order of households proposed by Kay is given in the first column. Households are ordered somewhat differently from Kay's original analysis because he did not have access to CA and used intuitive methods for the placement of households. It is interesting to note that in households that differed from the ideal pattern, the optimal score classification is different from Kay's placement. This is a nice illustration of the advantages of having an objective procedure for the classification of the nonideal types.

A special pattern emerges when the original data are rearranged according to the row and column optimal scores as in Table 7.3. To emphasize the pattern we have entered a 1 to indicate the presence of an item and a period otherwise. When ordered by CA in this fashion the 1's are maximally clustered as close as possible to the diagonal, whereas the periods occupy the off-diagonal areas. In fact, CA provides a weighted least-squares solution to this problem.

The arrangement displayed in Table 7.3 is the optimal ordering of both households and items along the continuum from "most" (in the upper left-hand corner) to "least" (in the lower right-hand corner). The row and column scores represent the "optimal" scale values for the various categories. In exploratory research it is frequently useful to examine the data ordered by the first row and column scores. The examination of the reordered data can frequently provide strong clues as to the nature of the structure of the data. It can reveal, for example,

TABLE 7.2

## Indicator Matrix Format Showing Presence (P) or Absence (A) of Seven Consumer Goods for 40 Papeete Households in Order Given by Kay (1964: 161-162)

| Auto | | Refrigerator | | Kerosene or Gas Stove | | 2-Wheeled Motor Vehicle | | Radio | | Bicycle | | Primus Stove | |
|---|---|---|---|---|---|---|---|---|---|---|---|---|---|
| P | A | P | A | P | A | P | A | P | A | P | A | P | A |
| 1 | 0 | 1 | 0 | 1 | 0 | 1 | 0 | 1 | 0 | 1 | 0 | 1 | 0 |
| 1 | 0 | 1 | 0 | 1 | 0 | 1 | 0 | 1 | 0 | 1 | 0 | 1 | 0 |
| 0 | 1 | 1 | 0 | 1 | 0 | 1 | 0 | 1 | 0 | 1 | 0 | 1 | 0 |
| 0 | 1 | 1 | 0 | 1 | 0 | 1 | 0 | 1 | 0 | 1 | 0 | 1 | 0 |
| 0 | 1 | 1 | 0 | 1 | 0 | 1 | 0 | 1 | 0 | 1 | 0 | 1 | 0 |
| 0 | 1 | 1 | 0 | 1 | 0 | 0 | 1 | 1 | 0 | 1 | 0 | 1 | 0 |
| 0 | 1 | 1 | 0 | 1 | 0 | 0 | 1 | 1 | 0 | 1 | 0 | 1 | 0 |
| 0 | 1 | 0 | 1 | 1 | 0 | 1 | 0 | 1 | 0 | 1 | 0 | 1 | 0 |
| 0 | 1 | 0 | 1 | 1 | 0 | 1 | 0 | 1 | 0 | 1 | 0 | 1 | 0 |
| 0 | 1 | 0 | 1 | 1 | 0 | 0 | 1 | 1 | 0 | 1 | 0 | 1 | 0 |
| 0 | 1 | 1 | 0 | 0 | 1 | 1 | 0 | 1 | 0 | 1 | 0 | 1 | 0 |
| 0 | 1 | 1 | 0 | 0 | 1 | 1 | 0 | 1 | 0 | 1 | 0 | 1 | 0 |
| 0 | 1 | 0 | 1 | 0 | 1 | 1 | 0 | 1 | 0 | 1 | 0 | 1 | 0 |
| 0 | 1 | 0 | 1 | 0 | 1 | 1 | 0 | 1 | 0 | 1 | 0 | 1 | 0 |
| 0 | 1 | 0 | 1 | 0 | 1 | 1 | 0 | 1 | 0 | 1 | 0 | 1 | 0 |
| 0 | 1 | 0 | 1 | 0 | 1 | 1 | 0 | 1 | 0 | 1 | 0 | 1 | 0 |
| 0 | 1 | 0 | 1 | 0 | 1 | 0 | 1 | 1 | 0 | 1 | 0 | 1 | 0 |
| 0 | 1 | 0 | 1 | 0 | 1 | 0 | 1 | 1 | 0 | 1 | 0 | 1 | 0 |
| 0 | 1 | 0 | 1 | 0 | 1 | 0 | 1 | 1 | 0 | 1 | 0 | 1 | 0 |
| 0 | 1 | 0 | 1 | 0 | 1 | 0 | 1 | 1 | 0 | 1 | 0 | 1 | 0 |
| 0 | 1 | 0 | 1 | 0 | 1 | 0 | 1 | 1 | 0 | 1 | 0 | 1 | 0 |
| 0 | 1 | 0 | 1 | 0 | 1 | 0 | 1 | 1 | 0 | 1 | 0 | 1 | 0 |
| 0 | 1 | 0 | 1 | 1 | 0 | 0 | 1 | 0 | 1 | 1 | 0 | 1 | 0 |
| 0 | 1 | 0 | 1 | 0 | 1 | 1 | 0 | 0 | 1 | 1 | 0 | 1 | 0 |
| 0 | 1 | 0 | 1 | 0 | 1 | 0 | 1 | 0 | 1 | 1 | 0 | 1 | 0 |
| 0 | 1 | 0 | 1 | 0 | 1 | 0 | 1 | 0 | 1 | 1 | 0 | 1 | 0 |
| 0 | 1 | 0 | 1 | 0 | 1 | 0 | 1 | 0 | 1 | 1 | 0 | 1 | 0 |
| 0 | 1 | 0 | 1 | 0 | 1 | 0 | 1 | 0 | 1 | 1 | 0 | 1 | 0 |
| 0 | 1 | 0 | 1 | 0 | 1 | 0 | 1 | 0 | 1 | 1 | 0 | 1 | 0 |
| 0 | 1 | 0 | 1 | 0 | 1 | 0 | 1 | 0 | 1 | 1 | 0 | 1 | 0 |
| 0 | 1 | 0 | 1 | 0 | 1 | 0 | 1 | 0 | 1 | 1 | 0 | 1 | 0 |
| 0 | 1 | 0 | 1 | 0 | 1 | 0 | 1 | 0 | 1 | 1 | 0 | 0 | 1 |
| 0 | 1 | 0 | 1 | 0 | 1 | 0 | 1 | 0 | 1 | 0 | 1 | 1 | 0 |
| 0 | 1 | 0 | 1 | 0 | 1 | 0 | 1 | 0 | 1 | 0 | 1 | 1 | 0 |
| 0 | 1 | 0 | 1 | 0 | 1 | 0 | 1 | 0 | 1 | 0 | 1 | 1 | 0 |
| 0 | 1 | 0 | 1 | 0 | 1 | 0 | 1 | 0 | 1 | 0 | 1 | 1 | 0 |
| 0 | 1 | 0 | 1 | 0 | 1 | 0 | 1 | 0 | 1 | 0 | 1 | 1 | 0 |
| 0 | 1 | 0 | 1 | 0 | 1 | 0 | 1 | 0 | 1 | 0 | 1 | 0 | 1 |

## TABLE 7.3

### Shows Results of Correspondence Analysis Applied to Durable Consumer Goods in 40 Papeete Households With Comparison of Scale Types Given by Kay

| Household | Automobile Through Primus Present | | | | | | | Automobile Through Primus Absent | | | | | | | Kay Type | Optimal Score |
|---|---|---|---|---|---|---|---|---|---|---|---|---|---|---|---|---|
| 1 | 1 | 1 | 1 | 1 | 1 | 1 | 1 | . | . | . | . | . | . | . | 7 | 1.874 |
| 2 | 1 | 1 | 1 | 1 | 1 | 1 | 1 | . | . | . | . | . | . | . | 7 | 1.874 |
| 3 | . | 1 | 1 | 1 | 1 | 1 | 1 | 1 | . | . | . | . | . | . | 6 | 1.225 |
| 4 | . | 1 | 1 | 1 | 1 | 1 | 1 | 1 | . | . | . | . | . | . | 6 | 1.225 |
| 5 | . | 1 | 1 | 1 | 1 | 1 | 1 | 1 | . | . | . | . | . | . | 6 | 1.225 |
| 6 | . | 1 | 1 | . | 1 | 1 | 1 | 1 | . | . | 1 | . | . | . | 6* | .812 |
| 7 | . | 1 | 1 | . | 1 | 1 | 1 | 1 | . | . | 1 | . | . | . | 6* | .812 |
| 11 | . | 1 | . | 1 | 1 | 1 | 1 | 1 | . | 1 | . | . | . | . | 4* | .784 |
| 12 | . | 1 | . | 1 | 1 | 1 | 1 | 1 | . | 1 | . | . | . | . | 4* | .784 |
| 8 | . | . | 1 | 1 | 1 | 1 | 1 | 1 | 1 | . | . | . | . | . | 5 | .724 |
| 9 | . | . | 1 | 1 | 1 | 1 | 1 | 1 | 1 | . | . | . | . | . | 5 | .724 |
| 10 | . | . | 1 | . | 1 | 1 | 1 | 1 | 1 | . | 1 | . | . | . | 5* | .311 |
| 13 | . | . | . | 1 | 1 | 1 | 1 | 1 | 1 | 1 | . | . | . | . | 4 | .283 |
| 14 | . | . | . | 1 | 1 | 1 | 1 | 1 | 1 | 1 | . | . | . | . | 4 | .283 |
| 15 | . | . | . | 1 | 1 | 1 | 1 | 1 | 1 | 1 | . | . | . | . | 4 | .283 |
| 16 | . | . | . | 1 | 1 | 1 | 1 | 1 | 1 | 1 | . | . | . | . | 4 | .283 |
| 23 | . | . | 1 | . | . | 1 | 1 | 1 | 1 | . | 1 | 1 | . | . | 2* | −.112 |
| 17 | . | . | . | 1 | 1 | 1 | 1 | 1 | 1 | 1 | 1 | . | . | . | 3 | −.130 |
| 18 | . | . | . | 1 | 1 | 1 | 1 | 1 | 1 | 1 | 1 | . | . | . | 3 | −.130 |
| 19 | . | . | . | 1 | 1 | 1 | 1 | 1 | 1 | 1 | 1 | . | . | . | 3 | −.130 |
| 20 | . | . | . | 1 | 1 | 1 | 1 | 1 | 1 | 1 | 1 | . | . | . | 3 | −.130 |
| 21 | . | . | . | 1 | 1 | 1 | 1 | 1 | 1 | 1 | 1 | . | . | . | 3 | −.130 |
| 22 | . | . | . | 1 | 1 | 1 | 1 | 1 | 1 | 1 | 1 | . | . | . | 3 | −.130 |
| 24 | . | . | . | 1 | . | 1 | 1 | 1 | 1 | . | 1 | . | . | . | 2* | −.140 |
| 25 | . | . | . | . | 1 | 1 | 1 | 1 | 1 | 1 | 1 | . | . | . | 2 | −.553 |
| 26 | . | . | . | . | 1 | 1 | 1 | 1 | 1 | 1 | 1 | . | . | . | 2 | −.553 |
| 27 | . | . | . | . | 1 | 1 | 1 | 1 | 1 | 1 | 1 | . | . | . | 2 | −.553 |
| 28 | . | . | . | . | 1 | 1 | 1 | 1 | 1 | 1 | 1 | . | . | . | 2 | −.553 |
| 29 | . | . | . | . | 1 | 1 | 1 | 1 | 1 | 1 | 1 | . | . | . | 2 | −.553 |
| 30 | . | . | . | . | 1 | 1 | 1 | 1 | 1 | 1 | 1 | . | . | . | 2 | −.553 |
| 31 | . | . | . | . | 1 | 1 | 1 | 1 | 1 | 1 | 1 | . | . | . | 2 | −.553 |
| 32 | . | . | . | . | 1 | 1 | 1 | 1 | 1 | 1 | 1 | . | . | . | 2 | −.553 |
| 33 | . | . | . | . | 1 | . | 1 | 1 | 1 | 1 | 1 | . | 1 | . | 2* | −.953 |
| 34 | . | . | . | . | . | . | 1 | 1 | 1 | 1 | 1 | 1 | 1 | . | 1 | −.957 |
| 35 | . | . | . | . | . | . | 1 | 1 | 1 | 1 | 1 | 1 | 1 | . | 1 | −.957 |
| 36 | . | . | . | . | . | . | 1 | 1 | 1 | 1 | 1 | 1 | 1 | . | 1 | −.957 |
| 37 | . | . | . | . | . | . | 1 | 1 | 1 | 1 | 1 | 1 | 1 | . | 1 | −.957 |
| 38 | . | . | . | . | . | . | 1 | 1 | 1 | 1 | 1 | 1 | 1 | . | 1 | −.957 |
| 39 | . | . | . | . | . | . | 1 | 1 | 1 | 1 | 1 | 1 | 1 | . | 1 | −.957 |
| 40 | . | . | . | . | . | . | . | 1 | 1 | 1 | 1 | 1 | 1 | 1 | 0 | −1.357 |

*Classification errors in Kay's original analysis.

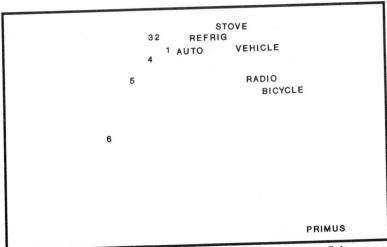

Figure 7.2.  Plot of Item Optimal Scores With Labels on Positive Columns and Numbers on Negative Columns

whether things are ordered along a single dimension, as in the present example, or whether a few distinct clusters are present, in which case there would be strong breaks visible between clusters.

## An Invariance Property of Multiple-Way Indicator Matrices

There is an important invariance property of certain transformations of indicator matrices that is also true of multiple-way indicator matrices of the kind shown in Table 7.2 above. A CA of a cross-product matrix gives identical row and column scores to those obtained from an analysis of the original indicator matrix. In CA, such a cross-product matrix is sometimes called a Burt matrix (Greenacre, 1984: 140+). The singular values from a cross-product matrix are the square of those obtained from the original matrix. Table 7.4 shows the Burt matrix obtained by multiplying the transpose of the indicator matrix by the indicator matrix.

Note that the matrix is symmetric with 14 rows and 14 columns. Along the diagonal of the matrix are seven two-by-two matrices with counts of "presence" of item in the upper left corner and counts of "absence" of item in the lower right corner and zeros in the off-diagonal

TABLE 7.4

Kay Data in Burt Matrix Form Obtained by
Multiplying the Transposed Kay Data by the Original Matrix.
Since the Matrix is Symmetric the Row Labels Are the
Same as the Column Labels.

| Auto | | Refrigerator | | Kerosene or Gas Stove | | 2-Wheeled Motor Vehicle | | Radio | | Bicycle | | Primus Stove | |
|---|---|---|---|---|---|---|---|---|---|---|---|---|---|
| P | A | P | A | P | A | P | A | P | A | P | A | P | A |
| 2 | 0 | 2 | 0 | 2 | 0 | 2 | 0 | 2 | 0 | 2 | 0 | 2 | 0 |
| 0 | 38 | 7 | 31 | 9 | 29 | 12 | 26 | 20 | 18 | 31 | 7 | 36 | 2 |
| 2 | 7 | 9 | 0 | 7 | 2 | 7 | 2 | 9 | 0 | 9 | 0 | 9 | 0 |
| 0 | 31 | 0 | 31 | 4 | 27 | 7 | 24 | 13 | 18 | 24 | 7 | 29 | 2 |
| 2 | 9 | 7 | 4 | 11 | 0 | 7 | 4 | 10 | 1 | 11 | 0 | 11 | 0 |
| 0 | 29 | 2 | 27 | 0 | 29 | 7 | 22 | 12 | 17 | 22 | 7 | 27 | 2 |
| 2 | 12 | 7 | 7 | 7 | 7 | 14 | 0 | 13 | 1 | 14 | 0 | 14 | 0 |
| 0 | 26 | 2 | 24 | 4 | 22 | 0 | 26 | 9 | 17 | 19 | 7 | 24 | 2 |
| 2 | 20 | 9 | 13 | 10 | 12 | 13 | 9 | 22 | 0 | 22 | 0 | 22 | 0 |
| 0 | 18 | 0 | 18 | 1 | 17 | 1 | 17 | 0 | 18 | 11 | 7 | 16 | 2 |
| 2 | 31 | 9 | 24 | 11 | 22 | 14 | 19 | 22 | 11 | 33 | 0 | 32 | 1 |
| 0 | 7 | 0 | 7 | 0 | 7 | 0 | 7 | 0 | 7 | 0 | 7 | 6 | 1 |
| 2 | 36 | 9 | 29 | 11 | 27 | 14 | 24 | 22 | 16 | 32 | 6 | 38 | 0 |
| 0 | 2 | 0 | 2 | 0 | 2 | 0 | 2 | 0 | 2 | 1 | 1 | 0 | 2 |

cells. These two-by-two matrices correspond to actual contingency tables between variables. Thus, for example, in the upper left we can see that just two households have an automobile and 38 households do not have an automobile. Similarly, in the lower right two-by-two matrix we see that 38 households have a primus stove and two do not.

Above the main diagonal are arranged 21 two-by-two contingency tables, one for each of the possible combinations of the seven items. Thus the whole table may be viewed as a collection of two-by-two contingency tables. They are arranged in such a way that both the row and column scores give results identical to the column scores of the indicator matrix. These scores represent the 14 variables composed of seven pairs of presence and absence of household durable consumer goods.

The use of multiple-way indicator matrices and Burt matrices is one kind of multiple correspondence analysis. Guttman scaling is but one example of a very specialized type of multiple correspondence analysis. In the next chapter we generalize to other applications of multiple correspondence analysis.

# 8. MULTIPLE CORRESPONDENCE ANALYSIS

There are two different approaches to generalizing CA to multiway data: multiple indicator matrices and stacking. Multiway data arise anytime we have more than two categorical variables. We might have, for example, types of crimes classified by city for a number of years. This is a three-way data matrix, crimes by city by year. We will describe the two analyses for this hypothetical example.

To perform an analysis on *indicator* data we would form a matrix in which the rows were each individual case (the unit of study) and the columns represented the crimes, cities, and years. There would be a separate column for each distinct category of each of the three variables. Each variable (crime, city, year) is classified into mutually exclusive and exhaustive categories, each of which gets a separate column. In this arrangement each row sums to exactly three (because there are three variables). This is exactly the format used in the Kay study on Guttman scaling (there, each of the seven variables had two categories). Similar rows can be, and usually are, added together prior to analysis. Assuming the main interest is in the types of crimes that occur differentially in the cities and years, one can calculate and plot an optimal score for each category of each variable in the same "space."

*Stacking* follows a completely different route to the description of multiway data. In this case we form a two-way contingency table of crimes by city for each year. One then forms a large matrix of data by simply putting the tables next to one another. If the crimes are rows, the cities are columns, and each table is a different year, then one large table can be created, that is: (1) the number of crimes *by* the number of cities times the number of years or (2) the number of crimes times the number of years *by* the number of cities. An analysis of the latter matrix allows for the calculation of a separate optimal score for each crime for each year. The examination of such a plot allows one to determine if crimes change by year. An analysis of the former matrix, with cities as rows, provides similar information for cities.

We have already seen an example of the multiway indicator approach in the last chapter in the Guttman scaling example. This method is appropriate for exploring the interrelations among true-false and multiple choice questions and can be extended to any number of categorical indicator variables. It may even be used with continuously measured variables by dividing them into categories. The number of categories per variable need not be the same so that variables with two, three, four, or more categories can be in the indicator matrix.

Stacking of a series of two-way tables is another approach to multiple correspondence analysis. If each two-way table represents a region, experimental condition, time period, and so on, then a simple correspondence analysis of the "stacked" matrix allows a direct comparison among regions, and so on. It is important to note that the ability to plot stacked replications is widely adaptable to a variety of situations. For example, the contraception example can be viewed as a series of stacked data matrices, four questions (availability, effectiveness, safety, and convenience) by gender (male, female). The optimal scores of these groups allow for comparisons within groups. Analysis of individually coded data would sacrifice simplicity but allow more detailed analysis of variability by gender or question. In the next section we illustrate an application of the method of multiple comparisons with "stacked" tables.

## Multiple Comparisons Using "Stacked" Matrices

Table 8.1 contains four 8 × 8 tables of judged similarity frequencies for a single set of objects, namely, kinship terms in English (Romney and D'Andrade, 1964). The first two tables were obtained from a triad test of judged similarities and represent the mean (means were used because the data are aggregated from different size groups) number of times a given pair of kinship terms is classed together, where six is the maximum possible score. Six has been added to the diagonal because we assume that an object is most similar to itself. The first set is based on 116 students collected at Stanford University, and the second set is based on 155 students collected at the University of California, Irvine. The third and fourth sets are deductions from two separate theories, namely, the Romney-D'Andrade and the Wallace-Atkins (see Wexler and Romney, 1972, for details).

A correspondence analysis of the combined (32 × 8) table will provide a visual representation of the similarities among the two sets of empirical data and the two theories simultaneously. Notice that there will be 32 row scores and 8 column scores. Each of the kinterms will appear four times in the row scores, one for each of the data sets. If in the spatial representation the points representing the two data sets are always close together it will demonstrate that the similarity structure is stable and can be replicated. The similarity or propinquity of the two theories to the data should indicate how adequately they represent the

TABLE 8.1

Similarities Among Male Kinterms from Stanford, Irvine, Romney-D'Andrade Theory, and Wallace-Atkins Theory

|  | GrFa | GrSo | Fa | So | Br | Un | Ne | Co |
|---|---|---|---|---|---|---|---|---|
| GrFa | 6.00 | 4.10 | 4.00 | 1.43 | 1.00 | 1.56 | 0.81 | 0.62 |
| GrSo | 4.10 | 6.00 | 1.62 | 3.17 | 1.55 | 0.77 | 1.68 | 1.10 |
| Fa | 4.00 | 1.62 | 6.00 | 3.80 | 2.32 | 1.95 | 0.61 | 0.55 |
| So | 1.43 | 3.17 | 3.80 | 6.00 | 3.68 | 0.63 | 1.23 | 1.43 |
| Br | 1.00 | 1.55 | 2.32 | 3.68 | 6.00 | 1.61 | 1.56 | 1.75 |
| Un | 1.56 | 0.77 | 1.95 | 0.63 | 1.61 | 6.00 | 3.71 | 3.48 |
| Ne | 0.81 | 1.68 | 0.61 | 1.23 | 1.56 | 3.71 | 6.00 | 4.24 |
| Co | 0.62 | 1.10 | 0.55 | 1.43 | 1.75 | 3.48 | 4.24 | 6.00 |
| GrFa | 6.00 | 4.25 | 4.50 | 2.31 | 1.01 | 0.92 | 0.31 | 0.27 |
| GrSo | 4.25 | 6.00 | 1.88 | 4.04 | 1.36 | 0.20 | 1.38 | 0.81 |
| Fa | 4.50 | 1.88 | 6.00 | 4.02 | 2.31 | 2.13 | 0.26 | 0.25 |
| So | 2.31 | 4.04 | 4.02 | 6.00 | 3.01 | 0.32 | 1.02 | 0.75 |
| Br | 1.01 | 1.36 | 2.31 | 3.01 | 6.00 | 2.47 | 1.63 | 1.75 |
| Un | 0.92 | 0.20 | 2.13 | 0.32 | 2.47 | 6.00 | 4.27 | 3.86 |
| Ne | 0.31 | 1.38 | 0.26 | 1.02 | 1.63 | 4.27 | 6.00 | 4.71 |
| Co | 0.27 | 0.81 | 0.25 | 0.75 | 1.75 | 3.86 | 4.71 | 6.00 |
| GrFa | 6.00 | 5.00 | 4.00 | 0.83 | 0.83 | 0.67 | 0.00 | 0.00 |
| GrSo | 5.00 | 6.00 | 0.83 | 4.00 | 0.83 | 0.00 | 0.67 | 0.00 |
| Fa | 4.00 | 0.83 | 6.00 | 3.33 | 3.83 | 3.50 | 0.33 | 0.50 |
| So | 0.83 | 4.00 | 3.33 | 6.00 | 3.83 | 0.33 | 3.50 | 0.50 |
| Br | 0.83 | 0.83 | 3.83 | 3.83 | 6.00 | 0.83 | 0.83 | 4.00 |
| Un | 0.67 | 0.00 | 3.50 | 0.33 | 0.83 | 6.00 | 4.33 | 4.33 |
| Ne | 0.00 | 0.67 | 0.33 | 3.50 | 0.83 | 4.33 | 6.00 | 4.33 |
| Co | 0.00 | 0.00 | 0.50 | 0.50 | 4.00 | 4.33 | 4.33 | 6.00 |
| GrFa | 6.00 | 0.33 | 5.50 | 0.50 | 0.50 | 3.00 | 0.00 | 0.33 |
| GrSo | 0.33 | 6.00 | 0.50 | 5.50 | 0.50 | 0.00 | 3.00 | 0.33 |
| Fa | 5.50 | 0.50 | 6.00 | 1.33 | 1.33 | 5.00 | 0.00 | 0.50 |
| So | 0.50 | 5.50 | 1.33 | 6.00 | 1.33 | 0.00 | 5.00 | 0.50 |
| Br | 0.50 | 0.50 | 1.33 | 1.33 | 6.00 | 4.50 | 4.50 | 5.00 |
| Un | 3.00 | 0.00 | 5.00 | 0.00 | 4.50 | 6.00 | 2.83 | 2.83 |
| Ne | 0.00 | 3.00 | 0.00 | 5.00 | 4.50 | 2.83 | 6.00 | 2.83 |
| Co | 0.33 | 0.33 | 0.50 | 0.50 | 5.00 | 2.83 | 2.83 | 6.00 |

data. The eight column scores will provide an aggregated, group picture of all eight kinterms.

In Figure 8.1 we have drawn lines (convex hulls) around all of the points representing each kinterm to aid description and interpretation. Note that the points representing the empirical data from the Stanford

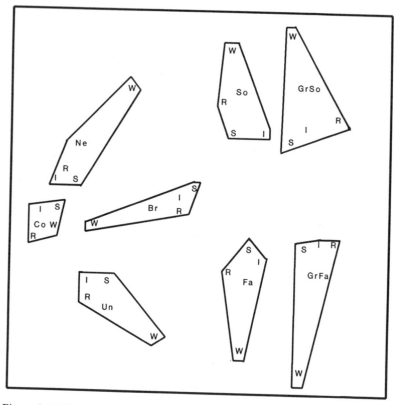

Figure 8.1. Plot derived from multiple correspondence scores of stacked matrices of judged similarity among eight male kinterms

Key: Kinterm abbreviations are aggregate scores from columns; from the rows, S indicates Stanford data, I indicates Irvine data, R indicates Romney-D'Andrade theory, and W indicates Wallace-Atkins theory. Points representing each term enclosed in convex hull.

and Irvine samples are close to each other for each of the eight kinterms. This indicates that the empirical structures are very similar with little sampling variability and can be expected to replicate from one study to the next. The empirical data are closely matched by the Romney-D'Andrade theory. This is a visual representation of the results reported by Wexler and Romney (1972) and Nakao and Romney (1984).

There are several aspects of this example that need further discussion. The idea of drawing convex hulls around replications of each point is a very powerful visual technique for obtaining an idea of how much variability there is among the individual cases. A visual examination makes it possible to identify outliers, as in the kinship example with the Wallace-Atkins theory, or whether a given point is less defined than others as indicated by an unusually large dispersion of individuals for the point.

We should note that, because the original data in this case are the mean number of responses, the inferential statistical tests described earlier are not applicable. It is helpful, nevertheless, to estimate goodness-of-fit between the data and the representation. Two sources of information can be used to make some estimates of how good the representation accounts for the data. The first information that should always be scanned is the (squared) singular values and the proportion each contributes to the sum of all values. As with PCA and MDPREF this ratio estimates the percentage of explained variance. There is no hard and fast rule about how large the first few singular values should be. In large and sparse tables, compared with small and dense tables, it is more difficult to account for a large percentage of the variance with few factors.

In the kinship example theoretical considerations lead us to believe that the data should be best described with three dimensions or factors: collaterality, generation, and reciprocity. The cumulative amount of explained variance as estimated by the squared singular values is 97.92% in three dimensions. The correlation between the reconstructed data and the original data is .956. (Goodness-of-fit estimates are presented in Table 8.2.) The correlation between two matrices is calculated by treating each as a vector and calculating the Pearson correlation coefficient. For each number of factors, a reconstruction of the matrix was obtained. Each reconstructed matrix was compared cell by cell with the original data in Table 8.1 to obtain the correlation reported in the last column of Table 8.2. The two-dimensional reconstructed data, represented in Figure 8.1, correlated .885 with the original data.

The correlations serve the same purpose as the so-called "Shepard" diagram does for nonmetric multidimensional scaling (Kruskal and Wish, 1978: 20-21; Schiffman, Reynolds, and Young, 1981: 136). These diagrams are monotonic scatter plots comparing the distances derived by MDS with the original values or proximities.

The analysis of stacked and combined tables of object by object proximities, as in this kinship example, has some strong relations to Individual Differences Scaling (Carroll and Chang, 1970; Kruskal and Wish, 1978: 60), a three-way multidimensional scaling technique for comparing individuals. The aggregate group picture given by the col-

TABLE 8.2

Some Descriptive Measures of the Adequacy of the
Correspondence Analysis for the Kinterm Data

| | Singular Values | | | Correlation Between |
| Factor | Value | Percent | Cumulative | Model and Data |
|---|---|---|---|---|
| $R_0$ | 1.000 | 61.32 | 61.32 | .153 |
| $R_1$ | .584 | 20.92 | 82.24 | .723 |
| $R_2$ | .415 | 10.56 | 92.80 | .885 |
| $R_3$ | .289 | 5.12 | 97.92 | .956 |
| $R_4$ | .184 | 2.08 | 100.00 | .983 |

umn scores in the CA is equivalent to the "group stimulus space" in
Individual Differences Scaling (INDSCAL). CA plots all the individual
pictures in the same space with multiple points given by the row scores,
whereas INDSCAL computes these separate pictures by weighting the
group stimulus space by each individual's weights.

It is also possible to correlate reconstructed scores with the original
data for each individual or group. This provides an idea of how well
each individual is fit by the model and would alert one to an individual
or replication that could not be accommodated in the model. In this case
the correlations are .94, .96, .93, and .95, respectively. These are very
close to the .955 for all individuals taken together. A related, and
sometimes more useful indicator, is the correlation of each individual
with the aggregated total. This measure is very sensitive to any case that
is fit well by the model but is not really like the other cases. These
correlations are: .97, .78, .95, and .69, respectively. Here we see that
the Wallace-Atkins theory correlates only .69 with the aggregate total
indicating that it is different from the two data sets and alternate theory,
a finding that reinforces the visual representation in Figure 8.1.

## A Few Final Words

In this monograph we have reviewed three methods of metric scaling.
These methods are adaptable over a wide range of data types and
research situations. In general any of the three methods may be applied
to the same data. With similar transformations applied to the data before
analysis they provide similar representations of the data. There are a

few situations in which each method has some special strength or weakness that should be pointed out explicitly.

Correspondence analysis is limited entirely to examining the association between the variables; differences in marginal totals are ignored. In ANOVA or log-linear model terminology, CA examines the "interaction" and ignores "main effects." When this interaction is the focus of the study and one wants to plot the row variables and the column variables in the same space it is probably the method of choice.

Sometimes the focus of attention is on the main effects or marginal totals, for example, the agreement among a set of subjects. Because this agreement produces very large differences among the column variable marginal totals (as there is agreement on the column variables) the main effects in the matrix are these marginal total differences. There may be little or no significant interaction. In these cases principal components analysis is clearly the method of choice. Frequently the first component summarizes this "magnitude" or "agreement" factor in a very useful way.

Multidimensional preference scaling parallels either CA or PCA depending upon the data transformations that are chosen. It represents both subjects (row variables) and items (column variables) in the same spatial configuration. When differences among marginal totals are removed MDPREF will provide a solution similar to that obtained with CA. When marginal differences are left confounded with the "interaction" between row and column variables, MDPREF results will parallel PCA.

All three methods are frequently found useful in situations that their developers did not anticipate and are far afield from original design purposes. All are very useful and adaptable tools for the description and analysis of data.


# APPENDIX
## Software for Metric Scaling

All analyses illustrated in this monograph can be performed on commercially available software. Data transformations, singular value decomposition (SVD), principal components analysis (PCA), multidimensional preference scaling (MDPREF), and optimal scaling/correspondence analysis (CA) are available with SCALER (Weller and Buchholtz, 1986). SCALER is available in executable FORTRAN and runs on an IBM-PC. MDPREF (mainframe version) can also be obtained from Bell Laboratories. ANTHROPAC (Borgatti, 1990) offers CA and runs on an IBM-PC.

Probably the most widely available source for PCA and CA is in BMDP (Dixon, Brown, Engelman, Hill, and Jennrich, 1988). BMDP runs on the IBM-PC and various mainframes.

# REFERENCES

ALDENDERFER, M. S., & BLASHFIELD, R. K. (1984) Cluster Analysis. Sage University Paper series on Quantitative Applications in the Social Sciences, 07-044. Beverly Hills, CA: Sage.

ARABIE, P. (1978) "Random versus rational strategies for initial configurations in nonmetric multidimensional scaling." Psychometrika 43:111-113.

ARABIE, P., CARROLL, J. D., & DeSARBO, W. S. (1987) Three-Way Scaling and Clustering. Sage University Paper series on Quantitative Applications in the Social Sciences, 07-065. Newbury Park, CA: Sage.

BATCHELDER, W. H., & ROMNEY, A. K. (1988) "Test theory without an answer key." Psychometrika, 53(1):71-92.

BELSLEY, D. A., KUH, E., & WELSCH, R. E. (1980) Regression Diagnostics: Identifying Influential Data and Sources of Collinearity. New York: John Wiley.

BENZECRI, J. P. (1969) "Statistical analysis as a tool to make patterns emerge from data," pp. 35-74 in S. Watanabe (ed.) Methodologies of Pattern Recognition. New York: Academic Press.

BISHOP, Y. M. M., FIENBERG, S. E., & HOLLAND, P. W. (1975) Discrete Multivariate Analysis: Theory and Practice. Cambridge: MIT Press.

BOORMAN, S. A., & WHITE, H. C. (1976) "Social structure from multiple networks. II. Role structures." American Journal of Sociology 81:1384-1446.

BORGATTI, S. P. (1990) ANTHROPAC. Available from the author, Department of Sociology, University of South Carolina, SC 29208.

BRAINERD. G. W. (1951) "The place of chronological ordering in archaeological analysis." American Antiquity 16:301-313.

BURT, C. (1937) "Correlations between persons." British Journal of Psychology 27:59-96.

CARROLL, J. D. (1972) "Individual differences and multidimensional scaling," in R. N. Shepard, A. K. Romney, & S. B. Nerlove (eds.) Multidimensional Scaling: Theory and Applications in the Behavioral Sciences (Vol. I). New York: Seminar Press.

CARROLL, J. D., & CHANG, J. J. (1970) "Analysis of individual differences in multidimensional scaling via an N-way generalization of 'Eckart-Young' decomposition." Psychometrika 35:283-319.

CARROLL, J. D., GREEN, P. E., & SCHAFFER, C. M. (1986) "Interpoint distance comparisons in correspondence analysis." Journal of Marketing Research 23:271-280.

CHANG, J. J., & CARROLL, J. D. (1968) How to use MDPREF, a computer program for multidimensional analysis of preference data. Unpublished Report, Bell Telephone Laboratories.

CHATFIELD, C., & COLLINS, A. J. (1980) Introduction to Multivariate Analysis. London: Chapman and Hall.

COOMBS, C. H. (1964) A Theory of Data. New York: John Wiley.

DIGBY, P. G. N., & KEMPTON, R. A. (1987) Multivariate Analysis of Ecological Communities. London: Chapman and Hall.

DIXON, W. J., BROWN, M. B., et al. (1979) BMDP-79: Biomedical Computer Programs P-Series. Los Angeles: University of California Press.

DIXON, W. J., BROWN, M. B., ENGELMAN, L., HILL, M. A., & JENNRICH, R. I. (1988) BMDP Statistical Software Manual (Vols. 1 and 2). Los Angeles: University of California Press.

DUNTEMAN, G. H. (1989) Principal Components Analysis. Sage University Paper series on Quantitative Applications in the Social Sciences, 07-069. Newbury Park, CA: Sage.

ECKART, C., & YOUNG, G. (1936) "The approximation of one matrix by another of lower rank." Psychometrika 1:211-218.

FIENBERG, S. E. (1980) The Analysis of Cross-Classified Categorical Data. Cambridge: MIT Press.

FISHER, R. A. (1940) "The precision of discriminant functions." Annals of Eugenics 10:422-429.

GILULA, Z. (1986) "Grouping and association in contingency tables: an exploratory canonical correlation approach." Journal of the American Statistical Association 81:773-779.

GILULA, Z., & HABERMAN, S. J. (1986) "Canonical analysis of contingency tables by maximum likelihood." Journal of the American Statistical Association 81:780-788.

GITTINS, R. (1980) Canonical Analysis: A Review with Applications in Ecology. Berlin: Springer-Verlag.

GOODMAN, L. A. (1979) "Simple models for the analysis of association in cross-classifications having ordered categories." Journal of the American Statistical Association 74:537-552.

GOODMAN, L. A. (1981) "Association models and canonical correlation in the analysis of cross-classifications having ordered categories." Journal of American Statistics Association 76(374):320-334.

GOODMAN, L. A. (1985) "The analysis of cross-classified data having ordered and/or unordered categories: Association models, correlation models, and asymmetry models for contingency tables with or without missing entries." The Annals of Statistics 13:10-69.

GREEN, P. E. (1973) "Multivariate procedures in the study of attitudes and asymmetry models for contingency tables status impressions." Social Science Research. 2:353-369.

GREEN, P. E., & CARROLL, J. D. (1976) Mathematical Tools for Applied Multivariate Analysis. New York: Academic Press.

GREENACRE, M. J. (1984) Theory and Application of Correspondence Analysis. New York: Academic Press.

GUTTMAN, L. (1941) "The quantification of a class of attributes: A theory and method of scale construction," pp. 319-348 in P. Horst et al. (eds.) The Prediction of Personal Adjustment. New York: The Social Science Research Council, Bulletin No. 48.

HABERMAN, S. J. (1974) "Log-linear models for frequency tables with ordered classifications." Biometrics 30:589-600.

HOLE, F., & SHAW, M. (1967) Computer Analysis of Chronological Seriation. Houston: Rice University Studies, Monograph in Archeology, Vol. 53.

94

HOTELLING, H. (1933) "Analysis of a complex of statistical variables into principal components." Journal of Educational Psychology 24:417-441, 498-520.

HOTELLING, H. (1935) "The most predictable criterion." Journal of Educational Psychology 26:139-142.

HOTELLING, H. (1936) "Relations between two sets of variates." Biometrika 28:321-377.

KAY, P. (1964) "A Guttman scale model of Tahitian consumer behavior." Southwestern Journal of Anthropology 20: 160-167.

KENDALL, M., & STUART, A. (1961) The Advanced Theory of Statistics (Vol. 2, 3rd ed.). London: Griffin.

KRUSKAL, J. B., & WISH, M. (1978) Multidimensional Scaling. Sage University Paper series on Quantitative Applications in the Social Sciences, 07-011. Beverly Hills, CA: Sage.

MARKS, W. B. (1965) Difference Spectra of the Visual Pigments in Single Goldfish Cones. Ph.D. dissertation, Johns Hopkins University.

McKEOWN, B., & THOMAS, D. (1988) Q Methodology. Sage University Paper series on Quantitative Applications in the Social Sciences, 07-066. Beverly Hills, CA: Sage.

MEZZICH, J. E., & SOLOMON, H. (1980) Taxonomy and Behavior Science. London: Academic Press.

MOSTELLER, F. (1968) "Association and estimation in contingency tables." Journal of the American Statistical Association 63:1-28.

NAKAO, K., & ROMNEY, A. K. (1984) "A method for testing alternative theories: An example from English kinship." American Anthropologist 86:668-673.

NISHISATO, S. (1980) Analysis of Categorical Data: Dual Scaling and Its Applications. Toronto: University of Toronto Press.

NISHISATO S., & SHEU, W. (1980) "Piecewise method of reciprocal averages for dual scaling of multiple-choice data." Psychometrika 45:467-478.

NUNALLY, J. C. (1978) Psychometric Theory. New York: McGraw-Hill.

ROMNEY, A. K., BATCHELDER, W. H., & WELLER, S. C. (1987) "Recent applications of cultural consensus theory." American Behavioral Scientist 3(2):163-177.

ROMNEY, A. K., & D'ANDRADE, R. G. (1964) "Cognitive aspects of English kinship." Special Publication, American Anthropologist 66(3, Part 2):146-170.

ROMNEY, A. K., WELLER, S. C., & BATCHELDER, W. H. (1986) "Culture as consensus: A theory of culture and informant accuracy." American Anthropologist 99(2):313-338.

SCHIFFMAN, H., & FALKENBERG, P. (1968) "The organization of stimuli and sensory neurons." Physiology and Behavior 3:197-201.

SCHIFFMAN, S. S., REYNOLDS, M. L., & YOUNG, F. W. (1981) Introduction to Multidimensional Scaling: Theory, Methods, and Applications. New York: Academic Press.

SNEATH, P. H. A., & SOKAL, R. R. (1973) Numerical Taxonomy: The Principles and Practice of Numerical Classification. San Francisco: Freeman.

SNEDECOR, G. W., & COCHRAN, W. G. (1972) Statistical Methods. Ames: Iowa State University Press.

SPEARMAN, C. (1904) "General intelligence, objectively determined and measures." American Journal of Psychology 15:201-293.

SROLE, L. et al. (1962) Mental Health in the Metropolis. New York: McGraw-Hill.

TENENHAUS, M., & YOUNG, F. W. (1985) "An analysis and synthesis of multiple correspondence analysis, optimal scaling, dual scaling, homogeneity analysis and other methods for quantifying categorical multivariate data." Psychometrika 50:91-119.

WASSERMAN, S. (1988) "Sequential social network data." Psychometrika 53:261-282.

WASSERMAN, S., & FAUST, K. (1989) "Canonical analysis of the composition and structure of social networks," pp. 1-42 in C. C. Clogg (ed.) Sociological Methodology. Cambridge, MA: Basil Blackwell.

WELLER, S. C. (1987) "Shared knowledge, intracultural variation and knowledge aggregation." American Behavioral Scientist 31(2):178-193.

WELLER, S. C., & BUCHHOLTZ, C. M. (1986) SCALER: A program to perform metric scaling. Available from the second author, Department of Preventive Medicine, University of Texas Medical Branch, Galveston, TX 77551

WEXLER, K. N., & ROMNEY, A. K. (1972) "Individual variations in cognitive structures," pp. 73-92 in A. K. Romney et al. (eds.) Multidimensional Scaling: Theory and Applications in the Behavioral Sciences (Vol. 2). New York: Seminar Press.

## ABOUT THE AUTHORS

SUSAN C. WELLER *is Associate Professor of Preventive Medicine and Community Health, in the Division of Sociomedical Sciences, at the University of Texas Medical Branch in Galveston. She received her Ph.D. in Social Sciences from the University of California, Irvine, in 1980. She has held faculty positions at the University of California, Irvine, and the University of Pennsylvania. Her research interests include scaling and clustering techniques and applications in the social sciences. She is especially interested in the measurement and representation of belief and attitudinal data. Recently, she authored another Sage monograph (with Romney):* Systematic Data Collection *(1988).*

A. KIMBALL ROMNEY *is Professor of Mathematical Social Science at the University of California, Irvine. His special interests include measurement and modeling in the social sciences with special reference to cognitive anthropology. Together with Roger Shepard and Sarah Nerlove he edited the pioneering two volume work* Multidimensional Scaling *(1972, Seminar Press). More recently, he has written a series of articles on consensus theory with Batchelder and Weller. He has taught at Chicago, Harvard, and Stanford and has over 60 publications to his credit.*